The
Mac mini Guidebook

A practical, hands-on book for everyone—including Windows users—moving to Apple's compact computer

David Coursey

Peachpit
Press

The Mac mini Guidebook

David Coursey

Peachpit Press
1249 Eighth Street
Berkeley, CA 94710
510/524-2178
800/283-9444
510/524-2221 (fax)
Find us on the World Wide Web at: www.peachpit.com

To report errors, please send a note to errata@peachpit.com

Peachpit is a division of Pearson Education

Project editor: Judy Ziajka
Production editor: Simmy Cover
Copy editor: Judy Ziajka
Tech editor: Clifford Colby
Compositor: Maureen Forys, Happenstance Type-O-Rama
Indexer: Karin Arrigoni
Cover design: Mimi Heft
Cover photography: Fred Johnson
Cover model: Elsa Geremew
Interior design: Kim Scott, with Maureen Forys

ISBN 0-321-35746-9

9 8 7 6 5 4 3 2 1

Printed and bound in the United States of America

This book is dedicated to my family and friends, especially to my wife, Elionora, and my children, Larry and Maureen—and also to everyone who still believes that small computers can make the world a better place. Many of these people use Macs.

Thank You...

Every book gets a page of thank-yous that is usually given the title "Acknowledgments," which to me sounds more clerical than grateful. As a second-time author, you, dear reader, get the benefit of my having thanked everyone the first time—making for a shorter list, or at least a list with fewer names.

For starters, all the people in the previous list, at least the ones I am still speaking to, are included by reference in this list.

This book is already dedicated to my famously understanding wife, Elionora Bjuhr, who was even mostly in a good mood during the weeks when I was writing between midnight and 6 a.m. If only I could have been in a good mood during that time, too.

The dedication also includes my children, who are in fact house cats. But Larry and Mo will be 19 soon, so they are never far from my thoughts. Or lap. Try writing a book with an Apple PowerBook and a 16-pound cat in your lap.

Special thanks to Lisa Halliday, who helped research the applications, write the descriptions, and create the figures for Chapter 10. Lisa and I have worked together for more than a decade, and she's also my best friend. She worked hard—though not tirelessly since she has a day job, too—helping with the product reviews in Chapter 10. This book was, in fact, my secret mission to get Lisa, a Windows-user/Mac-hater, to start using a Mac. She's just informed me that as her fee she will keep the PowerBook I loaned her. I guess my plan worked.

My friends at eWEEK.com, especially David Morgenstern, have been accommodating of my weird schedule during the preparation of this book. Nathalie Welch and Keri Walker at Apple deserve thanks for providing information and hardware.

Lois J. Breedlove, who now trains the journalists of the future, was my first print editor and deserves credit (or blame, depending on your view of my work) for what's happened during the nearly 25 years since.

I was shocked when, during planning for this book, my editor, Cliff Colby, told me that Peachpit publishes nearly 200 titles a year. I don't know how a staff that seems so small accomplishes so much. Yet they still have time to be nice, even patient, with their most disorganized authors. (Me, for example.)

The Peachpit crew has been great to work with, now on a second book. Special thanks to my friend Cliff and all the others at Peachpit who helped with this book, including Simmy Cover, Mimi Heft, Scott Cowlin, and Victor Gavenda.

Editor Judy Ziajka deserves special credit for turning my manuscript into something approaching the written English language, yet leaving it still sounding like I wrote it. She has been most tolerant of a process in which all the chapters were being written at the same time and then all arrived on her desk pretty much at once.

Thanks to Dr. George Reed for helping make this book possible.

Finally, thanks to you, the reader, and to all the people who have supported my projects over more than two decades.

About this book

This book was written entirely in Microsoft Word 2004 for Macintosh on a Mac mini and, occasionally, a PowerBook G4. Judy did her editing in Word 2000 for Windows, and we successfully passed the files back and forth many times. The production team at Peachpit Press works mostly on Macs.

Other software used in the preparation of this book includes Ambrosia Software's Snapz Pro X, which was used for all the screen shots. Cyberduck, a fine FTP client, handled uploads and downloads. Much of the text was run through Linguisoft's Grammarian style and grammar checker. NoteBook, from Circus Ponies, arrived in the nick of time to help with organizing the illustrations and writing captions, which were cut-and-pasted into the manuscript.

About the author

David Coursey has more than two decades' experience writing about computing and personal technology for print and online publications, including *Infoworld*, *PC Letter*, *Computerworld*, *PC World*, *Upside*, CNET.com, ZDnet.com, and eWEEK.com. He is also president of David Coursey Consulting, Inc., which provides editorial and advisory services to technology companies.

A Macintosh user since 1986, his first book for Peachpit Press was *Mac OS X for Windows Users: A Switchers' Guide*, published in 2003. Visit him online at www.coursey.com or send e-mail to coursey@mac.com.

Table of Contents

Chapter 4 Sharing Your Display, Keyboard, and Mouse   47

Chapter 5 Connecting Your Mac mini to the Internet   61

Chapter 10 Recommended Software   197

Appendix A Keyboard Shortcuts   235

Appendix B Resources   241

Read This First

This book is intended for Windows users who are considering or have already purchased an Apple Mac mini computer. It begins by describing what a Mac mini is—the first consumer Macintosh since the late 1990s that doesn't include a built-in display—and ends with descriptions of some of my favorite Mac applications.

I encourage you to start with the chapters that address your most urgent needs. If you've already decided to purchase a Mac mini and plan to use it side by side with a Windows PC, start with the discussion of sharing a display, keyboard, and mouse in Chapter 4, followed by networking in Chapter 6, printing in Chapter 7, and security in Chapter 8.

If you haven't already purchased a Mac mini, I recommend that you read Chapters 1 and 3 first. They introduce you to the Mac mini and explain how and where to purchase one. I then suggest reading Chapters 9 and 10 to familiarize yourself with Mac software, especially the collection that's included with the Mac mini.

Chapter 2 is a collection of frequently asked questions that summarizes and sometimes expands upon the other chapters. Chapter 8 is a visual tour of the Mac OS X 10.4 Tiger operating system specifically intended to help Windows users quickly orient themselves in Mac OS.

This book also includes two special features, neither part of the book itself but both valuable to readers:

All of the URLs listed in this book can be accessed at the book's Web site: www.peachpit.com/coursey. If the URLs change, the Web site will reflect those changes as I become aware of them. Bookmark this page, and you'll never have to manually enter a URL from this book.

Also, I will do my best to answer any and all reader questions. If something in the book doesn't make sense to you or is found to be incorrect, please tell me. I'll do my best to help solve the problems. I will post this information (or a link to it) on the Web site as well. I am not intending to become an all-purpose help desk—your best source for help is Apple's extensive Help system—but if you've tried everything else, I'm happy to lend a hand.

Thank you for purchasing this book and have fun with your Mac mini.

—David Coursey
  coursey@mac.com

1

BYODKM

BYODKM: These six letters describe what the Mac mini is all about as well as how it's different from every consumer Macintosh offered since 1998. If you understand these initials, you understand both the Mac mini and why so many people have fallen in love with it. It is BYODKM that helps make the Mac mini the least-expensive Macintosh ever, and the first Mac primarily designed with Microsoft Windows users in mind. If you are reading this book, you've doubtless succumbed to the Mac mini's considerable charm.

As you read this chapter, you will learn:

- What makes the Mac mini special.
- Why the Mac mini is good news for Windows users who want a Mac, too.
- The technical details of the Mac mini.

The letters *BYODKM* stand for "Bring your own display, keyboard, and mouse," a phrase coined by Apple Computer chairman Steve Jobs and used to introduce the Mac mini to an SRO crowd at the 2005 Macworld Expo in San Francisco.

Maybe the mnemonic is a bit precious, but not having these items—and assuming that the customer already owns them—is key to the Mac mini's magic. This is a machine intended not so much for Macintosh owners, but for those who call Microsoft Windows their computing home.

These are people who have been attracted to the Macintosh, perhaps because they already own an iPod. Or maybe they've heard how easy the iLife creative applications are to use. They may even be aware that Mac OS X is, compared to Microsoft Windows, the Fort Knox of computer security.

The thinking at Apple must be that if you offer these people an inexpensive Macintosh, some of them will buy one. A starting price of $499 is certainly attractive, and made possible by asking customers to BYODKM. For an additional $50, these customers can purchase a switch that allows their new Mac mini to share the keyboard, display, and mouse with the PC they are already using.

This is a book primarily aimed at Microsoft Windows users who have or may be about to purchase their first Macintosh, specifically a Mac mini. I will walk you completely through the selection and setup process, help you create a home network to take advantage of some cool Mac-specific features, guide you on a quick tour of Mac OS X 10.4 Tiger, and introduce you to some of my favorite applications for the Mac mini.

In this book, I will not be bashing Windows. Rather, I am assuming that you have a Windows machine that you want to keep using alongside your Mac mini. To help you, I'll also describe how to connect both computers to the same keyboard, display, and mouse, as well as how they can share the same Internet connection, printer, and files.

This is the setup I am using in my home office, giving me Macintosh computing because I want it and Windows computing because I need it. Windows and I have a complex love-hate relationship. But isn't that true for most Windows users?

 Links to all the URLs in this book may be found at www.peachpit.com/coursey.

Introducing the Mac mini

Since 1998, all consumer Macintosh computers have had one thing in common: They were all-in-one designs with built-in screens. The first Macintosh, introduced in 1984, was also an all-in-one box (**Figure 1.1**). Later Macs separated the system unit and screen. They were reunited with the unveiling of the original iMac, a machine that created quite a sensation and remains, after updates, in the Apple product line today (**Figures 1.2** and **1.3**).

Figure 1.1

This is the original Macintosh that started it all back in 1984. (Courtesy Apple Computer)

Figure 1.2

The original iMac, a design that came in a variety of colors. (Courtesy Apple Computer)

Figure 1.3

This is the current iMac, now called eMac, featuring a large flat-panel LCD screen and a much sleeker design made possible by the thin display. (Courtesy Apple Computer)

Putting the screen and the guts of the computer into the same box allowed Apple to create some revolutionary designs. For people who wanted a Mac as their primary computer, the all-in-one design was great.

But this design also made Macintosh computers expensive. In the PC world, you can buy a low-cost computer and use the monitor, keyboard, and mouse you already own. This makes upgrading a PC relatively inexpensive, as PC hardware evolves much more rapidly than monitor technology.

Windows users have found it hard to justify purchasing a Mac at the prices the all-in-ones fetch, especially when they have a perfectly good monitor already sitting on their desks (and no room to add an all-in-one Mac anyway).

Enter the Mac mini, the first Macintosh specifically designed to attract Microsoft Windows users (**Figure 1.4**). Not having a built-in screen allows the Mac mini to find a home in places all-in-one Macs only dreamed of going—such as on the desktops of die-hard Windows users, who can keep their current display, keyboard, and mouse and share them with the Mac mini. A simple switch allows users to go back and forth between the two machines, with no restarts required.

Figure 1.4
Apple's Mac mini, the most exciting new computer of the twenty-first century. (Courtesy Apple Computer)

In retrospect, the Mac mini design is so obvious that you wonder why no one at Apple thought of it sooner. In 2002, before iPod hysteria swept the nation, Apple ran a series of advertisements featuring people who left the Windows world for a Mac, thus finding happiness (and a place in television commercials). With 20/20 hindsight, the money spent on those "switcher" ads almost seems wasted. And it may have been, for while the ads were widely admired, Macintosh sales remained about the same as before.

Of course, back in 2002 all Apple had to offer Windows users were machines that included a big display, such as the iMac or the PC-sized Power Mac (**Figure 1.5**). These tried, essentially, to push the Windows PC right off the customer's desktop. This was not a battle Apple could win.

Figure 1.5
A Mac that looks like a PC. This is a Power Mac G5, a favorite of the graphic arts, publishing, and film/video production industries. (Courtesy Apple Computer)

Because the Mac mini is so tiny—measuring 6.5 x 6.5 x 2 inches and weighing less that three pounds—it can find a place on even the most crowded desk. It's pretty easy to hide if you don't want people at the office to know you've brought a Mac mini to work. But at home, who'd want to hide such a great-looking piece of anodized aluminum and white polycarbonate plastic?

While the Mac mini is most assuredly the low end of the Mac product line, it's no slouch. For the types of things most people do every day, it has plenty of power. To get the most out of a Mac mini, however, additional memory is required, but we'll get to that in a bit.

What's the big deal?

So how *do* you explain the number of people—including Windows-using professional cynics like myself—who fell in love with the Mac mini at first sight? Why do so many people smile when they see one? And why has it sparked so many people's imaginations?

To understand this, let me offer some "givens" about the state of the Windows world that should be factored into the Mac mini equation:

- Most people buy more computer horsepower than they need. They end up paying more for a home or small-business computer than they have to. People can pay less and still end up with a computer that does what they want.

- For several years, there hasn't been much reason for people to upgrade their Windows PC to a newer model, even though they might be willing to spend money given a good enough reason.

- Many people, while not disliking Microsoft, consider Windows to be a "necessary evil" and would use something "better" if it were available to them.

- All computers are too difficult to use. But Mac OS X is less clumsy than other operating systems.

- It's no fun to replace something—such as a recently upgraded LCD monitor—that still works just fine. Computers and monitors can be replaced separately, and probably should be.

- Home entertainment and creativity applications are important to consumers. Some people have put off buying a computer, digital camera, video camera, or similar product because they believe these products are too difficult to use.

- Being able to share a broadband connection among several computers in a home or small office is often enough reason to have the connection installed. Not having all the computers networked is a waste of money and a source of family friction.

- Many people are afraid of viruses and hackers and feel unable to adequately protect themselves.

- The sturdy Linux operating system remains in the news, generating a halo effect that touches all things based on the Unix operating system, including Mac OS X. Indeed, Mac OS X owes its inherent security and stability to its Unix roots.

- All most people do with their computers is browse the Internet, use e-mail, trade instant messages or chat with friends online, use a word processor and spreadsheet, and keep an address book and maybe a calendar. These tasks do not test even entry-level computers.

- People would like to have more fun with their computers.

Meeting the needs of Windows users

When taken as a whole—hardware, operating system, included software—the Mac mini does a very good job of addressing the issues important to Windows users. It is a Mac designed with the needs of Windows users firmly in mind:

- The Mac mini is a good match of price and value. It is fast enough to do what people most want to do with a computer.

- Mac OS X is both easier to use and more secure than Microsoft Windows.

- The Mac mini is an excellent upgrade that allows people with a PC that still works well enough to use the display, keyboard, and mouse they already own.

- Macintosh networking, using Apple's industry-standard AirPort Extreme technology, is easy to set up and use. It works as well with Windows machines as with Macs.

- The Mac mini is the natural add-on for someone who already owns an iPod and would like a computer for storing and sharing music.

- Apple provides the iLife suite of creativity applications with the Mac mini. This software, bundled for free with the Mac mini, would be worth several hundred dollars in the Windows world.

- If all a person wants to do with a Mac is edit home movies or digital still photographs, the Mac mini will do the job quite nicely.

- Besides creativity software, Apple provides other applications, including browser, calendar, address book, e-mail, instant messaging, conferencing, and even word processing and spread-sheet applications, with every Mac mini sold. All this free software means that customers may never need to buy anything more.

- Because Mac OS X is built atop a version of the Unix operating system, the Mac mini offers many of the same benefits as Linux, but with a better user interface and a much larger library of appli-cations to choose from.

- The Mac mini is easy to set up, easy to work with alongside a Windows computer, and fun to use.

- The Mac mini offers possibilities for special uses, for instance, as a server and even within automobiles, that make sense for a small, inexpensive, and "headless" (that is no screen, keyboard, or mouse) Macintosh.

And if you run Microsoft Office, you'll find the switch to the Mac mini nearly seamless. I'll touch on application compatibility later in this book, but upfront let me tell you that Microsoft Office for Mac is both very nice and completely file compatible with the version of Office you are running on your Windows machine.

Almost 100 percent of people who spend each day working in Microsoft Office on a Windows machine could do their work on a Mac.

The only difference they'd notice is that the Mac Office interface is more elegant and less cluttered than the Windows version.

 A friend who read a draft copy of this book asked if the statement about "completely file compatible" is 100 percent correct. Well, I have never had a reader tell me it isn't, and I have asked both Apple and Microsoft and received repeated assurances, but I am also open to the possibility that some macros, particularly Excel macros, may not work on the Mac. Most people, however, don't use macros and will never face this potential issue.

Thus, the Mac mini stacks up very nicely against the state of the computing world today. And with pricing starting at $499, what's not to like?

What I Am Using Right Now

This book is being written on the $599 Mac mini with an extra 256 MB of memory and the AirPort Extreme and Bluetooth wireless cards installed. As I'm using it, this Mac mini costs $773 at Apple's online store.

For a Windows PC, I am using a Dell Precision 470 desktop that cost a lot more than I really want to admit. It processes my words at precisely the same speed as the Mac mini. It is, however, connected to a very nice Dell 19-inch LCD monitor, a Microsoft keyboard, and a Logitech mouse or Kensington Expert Mouse trackball.

All these devices share the same screen, keyboard, and mouse thanks to an IOGEAR four-port switch, described in detail in Chapter 4. With the IOGEAR, I can change from one computer to any of the others with only four keystrokes—sure beats being surrounded by monitors.

Of course, most people don't need three and sometimes four computers sharing the same keyboard, video, and mouse like I do. The typical Mac mini customer needs only a two-port switch that makes it possible to connect just the Mac mini and a single Windows PC.

That's precisely what I am planning to do at my wife's desk, which is really too small for the Compaq PC and LCD monitor she's already using. Like many people, she'd like to use a Mac for some things, but *must* use a PC for others. It's sad, but true, that not all Windows software is available for the Mac.

This requirement of many people for Windows-only software also helped clamp a lid on the success of Apple's switcher ad campaign. Lots of people wanted to switch but quickly realized they couldn't. So instead of switchers, these people became "adders"—that is, once they found space on their desks for an all-in-one Mac. But now: Mac mini to the rescue.

The Mac mini by the Numbers— and What the Numbers Mean

The Mac mini comes in two models. They differ only in the speed of their PowerPC G4 processor chip and the size of the hard drive built into the computer. Otherwise, the two models are physically identical and share the same technical specifications.

This computer is called the Mac mini for a reason. It measures a diminutive 2 inches (5.08 cm) high, 6.5 inches (16.51 cm) wide, and 6.5 inches (16.51 cm) deep. The Mac mini weighs 2.9 pounds (1.32 kg).

This size allows the Mac mini to be right at home on the most crowded of desktops or in the tight spaces of a home entertainment center. It also makes the Mac mini an interesting carry-around computer, provided that you have a screen, keyboard, and mouse at your destination. There are Mac mini cases being marketed for people who want to take the computer with them.

 During the life of this book, it's possible that Apple will bump the Mac mini to faster processors or significantly change other specs. If that happens, I will put an update to this chapter on the book Web site: www.peachpit.com/coursey.

The Inside Scoop

Many people want to know what's going on inside their computers. Some Macs are very easy to open, but some—such as the Mac mini—require a bit of effort. You can damage the case if you aren't very careful and at least a little bit lucky. You also have to disassemble it to get at the interesting pieces, which has been done for you in **Figure 1.6** so you don't have to.

Figure 1.6

The inside of a Mac mini. (Courtesy Peter Belanger Photography)

Optical drive

Hard disk drive, in a mount that includes the speaker and fan

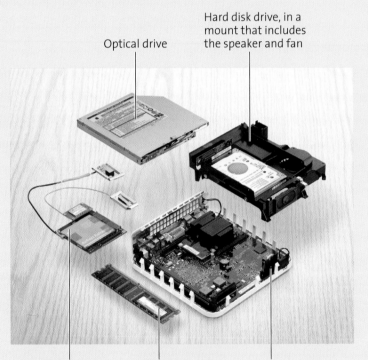

Wireless modules (the AirPort Extreme is the larger piece and Bluetooth the smaller); both are attached to small antennas

Memory module, which fits into a connector at the far left of the system board (next to the upward-pointing feet on the case)

System board, mounting into the case

Processor

The entry-level Mac mini is, as I write this, equipped with a 1.25 GHz PowerPC G4 processor, made by IBM. The other model has a 1.42 GHz processor.

If you come from a Windows PC background, I already know what you're thinking: "Geez, those minis are slow!" And compared to Intel and AMD processors cruising above 3 GHz, this would seem to be the case.

But sometimes things are not as they seem. And this is one of those occasions.

Processor speeds in the Mac and Windows worlds just don't compare evenly. The two operating systems, Mac OS X and Microsoft Windows XP, are just too different, and they accomplish the same things in different ways. That means that what a Mac does with 1 GHz takes a Windows machine... See, here I am, trying to compare directly—and it just can't be done. The temptation is great, nevertheless.

If the same application is running on both Windows and Mac OS machines, you can compare the time each computer takes to complete specific processing tasks. This approach is more useful than comparing the speed of an Intel or AMD processor to the Mac's PowerPC processor. It is also more useful for comparing one Mac to another.

Okay, let me go out on a limb: In practice, the Mac mini offers the sort of performance that an Intel Celeron-based PC provides. And this is plenty of horsepower for home and small-business users except those who already know—because they are graphic artists, programmers, professional film/video editors, and so on—that they need a faster Mac. Properly outfitted (that is, with more memory), I find the Mac mini's performance to be quite acceptable.

However, no Macintosh is truly a games machine. Yes, you can play games on a Mac, and there are some very nice ones available for Macintosh, but if your life is defined by the computer games you play...heck, you already know you need a souped-up $3,000 hot-rod PC.

Every Mac mini, as well as every other Mac, is equipped with something called a Velocity Engine. I don't think most Mac users have the vaguest idea what this is, so I looked it up. According to Apple:

The Velocity Engine, embodied in the G4 and G5 processors, expands the current PowerPC architecture through addition of a 128-bit vector execution unit that operates concurrently with existing integer and floating-point units. This provides for highly parallel operations, allowing for simultaneous execution of up to 16 operations in a single clock cycle. This new approach expands the processor's capabilities to concurrently address high-bandwidth data processing (such as streaming video) and the algorithmic intensive computations which today are handled off-chip by other devices, such as graphics, audio, and modem functions.

I am not a microprocessor engineer, nor do I harbor odd fantasies of becoming one. But that paragraph—there is a whole paper about this at Apple's Web site—helps explain why Intel's GHz and Apple's GHz cannot be directly compared. Visit developer.apple.com/hardware/ve/ to learn more.

The difference in processor speeds does show up in actual use, though it would be interesting to compare the impact of adding or not adding memory. There are other things to consider as well: specifically, slow hard drives, which we will come to later in this chapter.

Memory

Both Mac minis are equipped with 512 K of on-chip level-2 cache memory, running at full processor speed; a 167 MHz system bus; and 256 MB of PC2700 (333 MHz) DDR SDRAM, expandable to up to 1 GB.

Of this, the part that should concern you is the SDRAM. The consensus of people who write about Macs is that Apple is stingy with memory in its consumer models. Mac OS X is capable of running with this little memory, which is pretty impressive, actually—but adding more memory improves performance and allows the user to work comfortably in several applications at once.

Memory, however, is fairly inexpensive, and customers have shown a willingness to pay to add more memory on top of what the computer costs. So to keep base prices as low as possible—artificially low, some would say—Apple installs the bare minimum amount of RAM in its machines.

The Mac mini Apple sent as my review unit included an extra 256 MB of memory, bringing the total to 512 MB. This should be a very strong hint. However, if all you can afford is a 256 MB model, buy a Mac mini anyway. You can upgrade the memory later.

Memory compares fairly closely between Macs and PCs. Just as I want 512 MB or even 1 GB of RAM in my Windows machines, I also want 512 MB in my Macs, and 1 GB would be better, though installing that much memory in a Mac mini can be expensive.

Why? Because the Mac mini has only one memory slot, you must toss the existing memory in order to add more. And no, you don't have to buy your memory from Apple, though if you can afford to do so, this isn't a bad idea (more on this in Chapter 3).

Storage

The entry-level Mac mini is equipped with a 40 GB Ultra ATA hard disk drive. The more expensive model gets an 80 GB drive. There is no option to order a larger built-in drive. People shouldn't go tearing into their Mac minis just to install a larger hard drive. It is far better to add a USB 2.0 or FireWire external drive.

There is a beef with the built-in drives, however: They are slow, running at 4200 RPM. This is another of the compromises Apple made to reach a consumer-friendly price point. It's been noted, however, that some Mac minis have shipped with faster, 5400 RPM drives—alas, not including mine.

A faster drive can noticeably improve performance, but there is no easy way to determine the speed of your Mac mini's drive while you are still in the store, even if you power-on the machine.

Apple may offer larger drives in future Mac minis, though I suspect that the entry-level model will always have a small drive to match its small price. Perhaps someone will create an add-on drive in the same enclosure as the Mac mini itself, allowing the units to be stacked. Use a FireWire connection, and the external drive will seem plenty fast. Add more USB and FireWire ports to the add-on drive, and you will also have solved what may be my biggest complaint with the Mac mini: not enough expansion capability.

CDs and DVDs

The stock Mac mini comes with a slot-loading Combo drive (DVD-ROM/CD-RW) that reads DVDs at up to 8x speed, writes CD-R discs at up to 24x speed, writes CD-RW discs at up to 16x speed, and reads CDs at up to 24x speed.

You can replace this with the optional SuperDrive (DVD±RW/CD-RW). It writes DVD-R discs at up to 4x speed, writes DVD-RW discs at up to 2x speed, writes DVD+R discs at up to 4x speed, writes DVD+RW discs at up to 2.4x speed, reads DVDs at up to 8x speed, writes CD-R discs at up to 16x speed, writes CD-RW discs at up to 8x speed, and reads CDs at up to 24x speed.

Be thankful Apple selected a drive capable of burning both DVD-R and DVD+R disks. If your PC has a DVD burner, this allows you to standardize on a single type of disc.

Sounds like a Mac mini

Hopefully, the only time you will hear the Mac mini's built-in (and not so great) speaker is when the machine is first turned on and plays the startup sound. It's a pleasant sound, at least until you hear it coming out the air vents on the backside of your Mac mini the first thing in the morning (this seems a good enough reason to never turn off your Mac mini).

If you actually had to listen to this speaker for any length of time, it would surely damage your hearing. Okay, maybe it's not *that* bad, but you'll want a good set of speakers just the same.

On the Mac mini's rear panel, you will find a headphone/audio line-out jack, to which you connect a stereo mini-plug. Any decent pair of powered speakers will sound great with your Mac mini. You can also use this output, with a proper cable and adapter, to feed your home entertainment center.

Video and graphics support

The Mac mini includes an ATI Radeon 9200 graphics processor with AGP 4X support and 32 MB of dedicated double data rate (DDR) video memory.

One of the great things about the Mac mini is that is doesn't come with a built-in screen. Another is the broad range of screens you can connect to a Mac mini. For video-out, Apple wisely selected a DVI video output capable of digital resolutions up to 1920 x 1200 pixels. This supports the 20-inch Apple Cinema display and 23-inch Apple Cinema HD display, coherent digital displays up to 154 MHz, and noncoherent digital displays up to 135 MHz.

DVI is mostly important if you want to connect a Mac mini to a big screen monitor for home entertainment applications. There are, however, some newer LCD computer monitors (such as my Dell LCD) that feature DVI inputs.

Fortunately, a small adapter is included with every Mac mini, which turns DVI video into the VGA video output familiar to PC users. In VGA mode, the Mac mini supports analog resolutions up to 1920 x 1080 pixels.

If you have an older video projector or need support for other video output standards, S-video and composite video are available through the use of Apple's DVI-to-video adapter, sold separately.

Ports

There will be disagreement as to whether Apple included enough FireWire and USB ports on the Mac mini. I don't think so, though some users won't need more than are provided. Many Mac mini users will, however, end up with a USB hub, FireWire hub, or both, connected to their Mac mini.

The additional cost of a hub isn't huge, but these things add up. And these are attachments, adding more cables and power supplies to your Mac mini installation.

The Mac mini includes one FireWire 400 port and two USB 2.0 ports (**Figure 1.7**). These run at up to 480 Mbps. This is the same USB 2.0 that Windows machines use. FireWire is sometimes labeled IEEE 1394 on Windows machines.

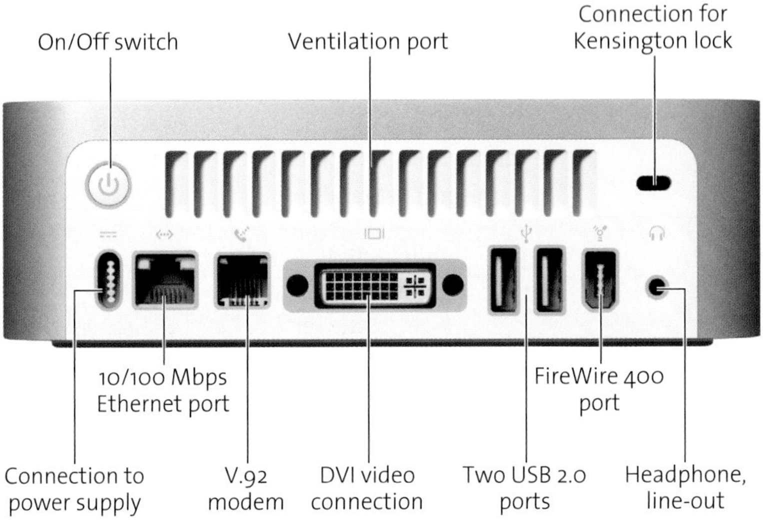

Figure 1.7
This is the rear panel of a Mac mini, with the various connectors marked. (Courtesy Apple Computer)

On/Off switch   Ventilation port   Connection for Kensington lock

10/100 Mbps Ethernet port   FireWire 400 port

Connection to power supply   V.92 modem   DVI video connection   Two USB 2.0 ports   Headphone, line-out

Here's how the ports are likely to be used:

- The FireWire port is where you're likely to connect an external hard drive, a video camera (for transferring movies for editing in iMovie), an iSight video camera for Web chats, an iPod, or an external hard drive.

- The USB port is where your USB keyboard and USB mouse will attach—using both ports. Or you can use a keyboard and mouse with PS/2 connectors along with a PS/2-to-USB adapter. These work fine (I am using one right now) and allow both the keyboard and mouse to share a single USB port. You can also use a USB port for attaching a hard drive, Web cam, iPod, or other peripheral device.

I hope Apple will provide more ports on future Mac minis. Someone moving from another Mac to the Mac mini or willing to buy the optional Bluetooth adapter and Apple's wireless keyboard and mouse *might* be able to get away with only three ports. But many Windows users, or anyone who really accessorizes their Mac mini, will need more.

Of course, to add these ports, a future Mac mini might also have to be a scoosh larger, which causes its own problems.

Communications

The Mac mini includes a built-in 56K V.92 modem that uses a standard RJ-11 telephone connector and built-in 10/100Base-T Ethernet adapter that uses a standard RJ-45 Ethernet connector. The modem is used to connect to the Internet over a dial-up connection.

The Ethernet adapter offers one method of connecting to broadband. The other is with the optional internal 54-Mbps AirPort Extreme card. It is based on the IEEE 802.11g standard and is Wi-Fi certified for 802.11g and 802.11b interoperability. This means that your AirPort Extreme card will work with any 802.11g or 802.11b network you may already own. I've tested with several vendors' hardware and have had no trouble connecting.

If, however, you haven't purchased a wireless network and go shopping, there are good reasons to buy an Apple AirPort Extreme wireless access point. I explain these in Chapter 5, but they revolve around ease of installation and setup and the use of Apple's AirPort Express devices for wireless printing and for extending your iTunes music collection to speakers in various locations around your home or to your home entertainment center.

Apple also offers an optional internal Bluetooth module, mostly useful for connecting to Apple's wireless keyboard and mouse and certain cellular telephones, handheld computers, and wireless handsets.

Bluetooth has been around for a while now and has tremendous potential to wirelessly replace the cables used to tie peripheral devices to computers, especially those that are connected only occasionally. But little of this potential has been realized, and I am inclined to give Bluetooth less consideration than it may actually deserve. So take my Bluetooth comments as those of a disillusioned user.

Electrical requirements

The Mac mini is powered by an external power supply and is Energy Star compliant. The computer can use as much as 85 watts of continuous power, provided by a power supply measuring 6.5 x 2.5 x 1.5 inches and swathed in Apple's signature white plastic. The power supply is not a "wall wart" that hangs from an electrical outlet, but is attached on one side to a power cord that plugs into the wall and on the other side to a cord that connects to a tiny power jack on the rear panel of the Mac mini. The power supply gets warm to the touch.

 The Mac mini power supply connector is very similar to that used by some of Apple's large monitors. Be sure not to accidentally connect the Mac mini to one of those.

At the end of the Mac mini's technical specifications is a list of operating temperatures and such that I won't bore you with. But one of the specs caught my eye:

• Maximum altitude: 10,000 feet

I understand that if you block the vent ports or set the Mac mini on top of a heating vent, it might cause problems. But what about elevation? Do computers get altitude sickness?

I am thinking about taking a Mac mini to Yosemite to see if elevation really matters. I wonder what happens to a Mac mini at 11,000 or 12,000 feet? I know I get a bit of altitude sickness, but will my Mac mini? Does its silicon brain go as simple as my gray matter brain does at altitude? Maybe so.

2

Mac mini Q&A

Macintosh computing is supposed to be simple, but books are supposed to be detailed, and that level of detail can sometimes make Mac computing seem complex. In an attempt at atonement, I offer this chapter to the Macintosh god.

As you read this chapter, you will learn:

- Answers to some common questions about the Mac mini.

- In a nutshell, what the rest of this book covers.

In this chapter, you will find the essential knowledge contained in the rest of the book—well, almost—written in shorthand form. The questions are organized into sections that correspond to chapters in the text, starting with Chapter 3.

Which Mac mini to Buy (and Where to Buy It)

For more information on the topics in this section, see Chapter 3.

Which Mac mini should I buy?

Unless you are absolutely cash strapped, I recommend that you spend the extra $100 and get the larger hard drive and slightly faster processor in the $599 model. You might not notice the speed bump, but as your music and photo collections grow, you will appreciate having double the hard drive space. If you are thinking about editing home video or using your Mac mini to record and store TV programs, the extra hard drive space is essential.

Do I need to buy additional memory?

Apple's upgrade from 256 to 512 MB costs $75 and is worth the money, if you can possibly afford it. The additional 256 MB of memory improves performance and allows you to have multiple programs open at once without bringing your Mac mini to its knees.

Increasing the memory to 1 GB, however, costs $325, which seems expensive, especially when you can order the memory online for about $160.

It's best to buy the memory you need when you purchase the computer, but you can make a change later. You will then have to either pay to have it installed or, if you feel up to the task, open your Mac mini's case and install it yourself.

The Mac mini has only a single memory slot, so if you upgrade you will find yourself left with the memory you removed. Maybe you can sell it on eBay. Probably not.

So do I buy the faster machine or more memory if I can afford only one?

Well, you can add the memory later for $75, but you can't change the hard drive or processor short of buying a new Mac mini. Let that be your guide. If you really will invest the $75 later for more memory, buy the faster machine. If not, I'd rather own the slower machine with the smaller hard drive but have the additional memory.

Must I buy memory from Apple?

No. The Mac mini uses standard memory that's widely available from a variety of sources. Check the magazines and Web sites listed in Appendix B.

Be sure to hold onto the old memory you remove, though, since Apple may not be happy to see third-party memory if you bring in the machine for repair.

Can I install the memory myself?

Yes. Do I recommend it? Not really. First, you have to open the Mac mini's case, an exercise that requires a pair of thin-bladed putty knives and a bit of skill. After that, you have to remove the memory from the Mac mini's lone memory socket and replace it with the new memory.

If you are comfortable opening other computers and installing memory, you'll be able to do this. Just make sure the upgrade you plan to do won't void your warranty. But if the thought of applying a flat blade to your Mac mini gives you vapors, then have Apple install the memory for you.

For directions on opening the Mac mini, do a Google search or visit *Macworld* magazine's Web site (www.macworld.com). I don't want to be responsible if you mess up the case.

Can I install an AirPort Extreme card and Bluetooth myself?

Apple strongly recommends buying your Mac mini with the wireless card installed at the factory. Apple does not recommend this as a do-it-yourself project. Although the memory socket is easily accessible, the wireless modules are not. I've played with a Mac mini motherboard— and you don't want to.

If for some reason you need to add Bluetooth, you can easily do this with a USB Bluetooth adapter. I am not aware of any USB 802.11 wireless adapters that work with the Mac mini.

Can I install a larger hard drive myself?

This is even less recommended than installing a wireless card yourself, but at least I can understand why someone might want to. The better route is to add an external drive, though adding a USB or FireWire external drive does add another box to your Mac mini installation. Yes, I wish Apple offered options for larger hard drives.

What is the recommended configuration?

If I were buying someone a present, I'd purchase the $599 model, bring the memory up to 512 MB, and replace the stock Combo drive with the DVD-burning SuperDrive. I'd also buy the AirPort Extreme card unless I was positive it would never be used—broadband and wireless just go together. I would also buy the Bluetooth adapter because it's only $20 additional and could conceivably be useful some day.

I would make sure my recipient had both a USB keyboard and mouse of the wired persuasion. If not, I'd buy them, expecting to pay $50, plus or minus a bit. I would not buy the Apple keyboard and mouse. If the person doesn't already own a display, the deal's off because I'm not buying one. Or maybe I will buy an eMac instead.

For a KVM switch, I have become very partial to the IOGEAR products discussed in Chapter 4. I paid about $60 for one at Best Buy.

Total value of this gift: $873, or $674 without the SuperDrive and wireless card. Now add $60 for the KVM switch and maybe $50 for a non-Apple USB keyboard and mouse. This brings the price to $983 or $785, respectively.

Buying an AirPort Extreme Base Station adds $199, and including the AirPort Express Base Station to be used with it to play iTunes on remote speakers increases the cost by another $129. If you don't care about iTunes, any 802.11g wireless base station will work fine.

Who should *not* buy a Mac mini?

The Mac mini is a great computer—but it is still a low-cost, entry-level machine. It does a lot for the money and comes equipped with some great software. But if you expect a Mac mini to perform like a $2,999 dual-processor Power Mac G5, you will be disappointed.

There are very few things that other Macs can do that a Mac mini can't do. But there is a difference between mere doing and doing quickly or well. For example, if I were a professional graphic designer, I'd buy a professional tool and invest in a more powerful Mac. I'd also buy one of those gorgeous Apple 30-inch LCD panel displays. I'd probably also end up spending about $6,600—plus a little more for some added memory.

But I am not a graphics professional, and for my amateur projects, the Mac mini gets the job done. Likewise with video. You can edit short videos on a Mac mini, but the Mac mini isn't suitable for professional editing. There are several reasons for this, not the least of which are the slow, single processor; the slow, relatively small hard drive; and the lack of expandability.

Is the Mac mini just an eMac or iBook minus the screen?

I don't want to cast aspersions, but let's compare the technical specs of a Mac mini to the eMac, the all-in-one Mac designed for the education market, and the low-end iBook G4, popular with students. I think **Table 2.1** speaks for itself.

Consumer	Mac mini	eMac	iMac G5	iBook G4
CPU	1.25 GHz PowerPC G4	1.25 GHz PowerPC G4	1.6 GHz PowerPC G5	1.25 GHz PowerPC G4
System Bus	167 MHz	167 MHz	533 MHz	133 MHz
Built-in Graphics	ATI Radeon 9200, 32 MB dedicated DDR SDRAM video memory	ATI Radeon 9200, 32 MB dedicated DDR SDRAM video memory	NVIDIA GeForce FX 5200 Ultra, 64 MB video memory	ATI Mobility Radeon 9200, 32 MB dedicated DDR video memory
Built-in Display	None	17-inch flat CRT	17-inch widescreen LCD	12-inch TFT LCD
Ports	One FireWire 400 port, two USB 2.0 ports, DVI output, VGA output with included adapter	Two FireWire 400 ports, three USB 2.0 ports, two USB 1.1 ports (on keyboard), mini VGA output port	Two FireWire 400 ports, three USB 2.0 ports, two USB 1.1 ports (on keyboard), VGA output, S-Video output, composite video output	One FireWire 400 port, two USB 2.0 ports, VGA output, S-Video output, composite video output
Networking	Built-in 10/100BASE-T Ethernet, 56K V.92 modem	Built-in 10/100BASE-T Ethernet, 56K V.92 modem	Built-in 10/100BASE-T Ethernet, 56K V.92 modem	Built-in 10/100BASE-T Ethernet, 56K V.92 modem, built-in AirPort Extreme

Table 2.1 The Mac mini has much in common with the eMac, an all-in-one machine designed for use in schools but also available for home users. The low-end Mac mini is better equipped than the entry-level iBook portable.

Now I'm not saying that the $499 1.25 GHz Mac mini is essentially a heavy eMac without the screen. Draw your own conclusions.

One of which should be that if you don't own a monitor and aren't planning to use your new Mac as a media center feeding your TV set, then an eMac might be a better deal for you. Fortunately, much of what's in this book applies to either a Mac mini or an eMac. Just skip Chapter 4, at least the part about KVM switches.

Sharing Your Display, Keyboard, and Mouse

For more information on the topics in this section, see Chapter 4.

Can I use the mouse and keyboard I already own?

In a word, yes. But it's best if you already own a USB mouse and keyboard. Chapter 4 explains how to share a PS/2 mouse and keyboard as well.

What's a KVM switch?

A keyboard, video, and mouse—or KVM—switch allows your Mac mini and Windows PC to share the same keyboard, video display, and mouse. KVM switches are available in models that switch from two to dozens—even hundreds—of machines.

KVM switches can be expensive, especially when the necessary cables are purchased separately. Some recent KVM switches are built with the output cables attached. Although this places a limit on how far apart your Mac mini and PC can be, it also significantly reduces the total cost of a KVM switch.

KVM switches come in two varieties, based on the type of input and output connectors they offer for the keyboard and mouse. These are PS/2 and USB. PS/2 is the standard PC keyboard and mouse connector. USB switches use the universal serial bus connector common on both PCs and Macs.

Does the Mac mini accept PS/2?

No. The Mac mini has two USB jacks, however. If you want to use your existing PS/2 keyboard and mouse, buy a PS/2 KVM switch and a PS/2-to-USB adapter, which accepts the PS/2 keyboard and mouse and combines them into a single USB output that plugs into the Mac mini. The adapter costs $25.

What switch and other gear should I buy?

My recommendation is to toss the PS/2 mouse and keyboard that came with your PC and buy a wired USB keyboard and mouse. Use these with a USB KVM switch that features built-in cables. I like the IOGEAR mentioned in Chapter 4, but the Belkin with the built-in USB hub is nice, too. It requires cables, however, as does a Belkin switch that uses DVI connectors.

Should I use DVI?

DVI, for digital video interface, is the native video output used by the Mac mini. Most users will install the supplied VGA-to-DVI adapter and connect a PC VGA monitor instead.

However, if you are connecting your Mac mini to a home entertainment center, you will probably use the DVI adapter (see "How to Turn Your Mac mini into a Media Center" in Chapter 9).

Also, some PCs and LCD monitors are being delivered with DVI connections. In my testing with a Dell PC, Dell flat-panel display, and Mac mini, I didn't see a significant difference between VGA and DVI.

Do I need to buy hubs?

The Mac mini is equipped with two USB 2.0 ports and one FireWire 400 port. This will be a significant limitation for some users. Fortunately, you can buy add-on hubs to expand the number of available ports.

If you add peripherals, expect to buy a USB hub, FireWire hub, or both. Or buy a combination hub, such as the one IOGEAR sent me to play with. But be aware that many hubs (including the IOGEAR) don't provide enough power to operate an Apple iSight camera or charge an iPod. These will end up plugged into the Mac mini itself.

Apple really needs to add more ports to the Mac mini.

Connecting Your Mac mini to the Internet

For more information on the topics in this section, see Chapter 5.

Do I need broadband to enjoy my Mac mini?

No, but broadband makes the Internet much more enjoyable.

I strongly recommend a broadband connection and a wireless network if you can afford them.

Can I hook up a wireless network myself?

Yes—and this is mostly what Chapter 5 is about. (The only reason to set up a wired network is when your Mac mini and PC sit side by side and you have no other computers to connect. In this case, you are sharing the same Internet connection more than creating a home network.)

The best plan is to order cable modem or DSL service and get these running on the PC. Then connect an AirPort Extreme Base Station to your cable or DSL modem instead of the PC.

Now turn on your wireless-equipped Mac mini and run the AirPort Setup Utility. Once your Mac mini is connected to the AirPort Extreme Base Station and seems happy, install an 802.11b USB wireless adapter on the PC and give it the name of your wireless network and its password.

It really should be that simple. You really can do it, even if parts of Chapter 5 might make you think otherwise. Trust me. I'll even give you my e-mail address, in case you need help. It's coursey@mac.com.

Should I replace my current wireless base station?

To use the advanced features of the $129 AirPort Express Base Station, which include printer sharing and the ability to connect powered speakers (or a stereo) and play iTunes music wirelessly throughout the house, I swapped my Microsoft base station for Apple's $199 AirPort Extreme Base Station.

I like the AirPort Express Base Station so much that during the course of writing this book I've purchased three of them.

How far will my wireless network reach?

Typically, a wireless connection works within 50 to 300 feet of a base station, with the connection becoming slower the farther from the base station you are. The distance covered may be 300 feet in an open field, but sometimes it's impossible to get a base station to cover an entire house. Fortunately, AirPort Express Base Stations can be used to extend a wireless network out from the main base station. Read Chapter 5 for details.

Printing with Your Mac mini

For more information on the topics in this section, see Chapter 6.

How do I share a printer between my Mac mini and my Windows PC?

AirPort Express is my preferred means of printer sharing—that is, if you don't want to have to swap USB cables whenever you want to print on the "other" machine. Yes, I did break down and buy a USB switch (IOGEAR again), and it is an option if you'd rather not reach behind your Mac mini so much. Most PCs now have USB ports on both their front and back sides.

I also have a printer with both an old-style Centronics connector running to the PC and a USB cable running to the Mac. Chapter 6 contains a handful of printer sharing ideas and alternatives.

Will all printers work with the Mac mini?

No, though most will. The Mac mini comes with 250 sets of printer drivers installed, covering most of the major brands. You can check the list on the Apple Web site (the link is in Chapter 4 or can be found at www.peachpit.com/coursey along with all the other links in this book).

If you are buying a printer, make sure it has Mac OS X drivers. Usually there will be a Mac logo on the box, but you can also check either the Apple list or the printer manufacturer's Web site.

The major brands (Epson, Canon, and Hewlett-Packard for example) all have Mac drivers for almost all their desktop printers, but some smaller manufacturers don't. I've yet to get my Konica/Minolta/QMS color laser printer to work with any Mac, for example.

What are Rendezvous and Bonjour?

In Mac OS X 10.4 Tiger, the technology formerly called Rendezvous became the equally dopey-named Bonjour. Because of this, you will see the two names used together for a while. And it may be a while before Rendezvous for Windows becomes Bonjour for Windows.

Rendezvous/Bonjour is technology that allows devices (such as printers), applications (instant messaging, for example), and computers to find one another and automatically create connections over an office or home network. It's very cool, but not as widely used as it deserves to be. Apple has written a version for Windows, especially useful for connecting to a shared Rendezvous/Bonjour printer connected to an AirPort Express Base Station.

Protecting Your Mac mini

For more information on the topics in this section, see Chapter 7.

How safe is the Mac mini?

As I write this—and for several years prior—Macintosh security vendors have been selling software that prevents only nonexistent threats. And they've been charging a lot of money for it, too. On this basis, I'd say the Mac mini is very safe, but that will probably change someday, perhaps even between the time I write this book and the time you read it. So some degree of protection makes sense.

What should my security strategy be?

Even with the absence of threats, I cannot recommend running a Mac without antivirus software. But whichever product you find for the least money is probably the best choice. I use Virex, which is part of the .Mac service for the earlier Mac OS X 10.3 Panther operating system (Virex does not currently run on Mac OS X 10.4 Tiger), and Norton security products on others. I hear good things about the Intego products as well, but don't have the many years' experience with them that I do with the others.

At the beginning of Chapter 7 are some quick-and-easy security tips. If you don't read any of the rest of that chapter, be sure to implement these suggestions. Some of them are very important.

What about phishing?

Phishing, which is the attempt to get someone's personal information (for identity theft) by sending a bogus e-mail claiming to be from a bank or other institution, is the most difficult security problem to handle. It's difficult for a computer to keep the unsuspecting from being swindled. But there will be improvements over time to ensure that mail really is from whomever it claims to be from and that Web sites really belong to their supposed owners.

Those of us who understand the phishing risk should warn our friends and family (especially seniors) to never give out personal information to someone who asks for it online.

How is most data lost?

Glad you asked. Most data isn't lost to external threats. It's lost because a file was accidentally erased or a hard drive crashed. For this reason, it's essential to back up the data stored on your hard drive.

My preferred solution is to use a backup program (such as .Mac's Backup or the lowest-end version of Retrospect) to back up onto an external hard drive connected to the Mac mini. Occasionally, I will make a DVD backup. And copies of my most important and/or commonly used files might be found on my online iDisk and an iPod or USB flash drive as well.

A Visual Tour of Mac OS X Tiger

For more information on the topics in this section, see Chapter 8.

How are Mac OS X and Windows different?

At one level, let me count the ways. But at another, they are both operating systems and offer the same features and functionality, just presented a little differently.

To me, the main difference is philosophical: Mac OS X sometimes trades off functionality in favor of ease of use. A Mac is very easy to use when Apple wants users to be able to do something—print, for example—but at some point, features just seem to stop. On the Mac, performing a task goes from easy to impossible in no time at all.

Windows, by comparison, tries to do everything you might want—and lots you never will. The common tasks are easy, but the more esoteric a job is, the more difficult Windows functionality can become. Windows users tend to interact with the guts of their operating system more than Macintosh users do.

How do I learn to operate a Mac mini?

In my previous book, written for people switching from Windows to Mac systems, I went to probably excessive lengths to explain the Mac OS to Windows users. In this book, I have tried to include just enough information to make readers feel comfortable sitting down in front of Mac OS X and exploring the Mac mini.

I think you can learn the basics of the Mac mini in about two hours. There's not much you can do to mess up the machine (unless you start messing around in the Utilities folder, that is), so go ahead and have fun.

Regarding the new features in Tiger: I am a big fan of the Spotlight search feature, which has already significantly changed how I use my computer. Generally, I've stopped trying to find lost files or e-mails "the old way" (manually) and now just type what I am looking for into a Spotlight search.

Dashboard, which provides useful small applications that can be accessed easily from just about anywhere on the system, is interesting, especially if Apple can convince third-party developers to support it.

Applications for the Mac mini and Recommended Software

For more information on the topics in this section, see Chapters 9 and 10.

How much software do I need to buy?

Between the software that comes free with the Mac mini and a $99 .Mac membership, I am not certain you need to buy any additional software. What the .Mac membership gives you, besides an e-mail account that you may not need, is backup software and an online iDisk where you can stash some important files. You also get .Mac Sync, which can serve as a backup but is most useful for keeping data synchronized across several Macs.

How does Microsoft Office for Macintosh differ from the Windows version?

The great thing about Microsoft Office for Macintosh is its compatibility with the Windows version. I have never run into a serious compatibility issue.

The worst thing about Microsoft Office for Macintosh is that it offers a program called Entourage as a weak replacement for the Windows-only Outlook. Entourage is useful mostly if you need to connect to a Microsoft Exchange server at work. It's not at all a bad program and works great with other types of e-mail accounts.

Since I have AppleWorks, do I need Microsoft Office?

Certainly, you should try AppleWorks, the Microsoft Office–like set of programs that comes free with the Mac mini. It is not nearly as full featured as Office, but if it works for you, you've saved some money. If not, Microsoft Office is the way to go.

What software do you recommend for a home office?

I'd buy Microsoft Office, at the discounted student pricing if I qualified, for the word processing and spreadsheet applications. I'd use the free Mail, Address Book, and iCal applications that come with the Mac mini for those features.

For small business accounting, there's QuickBooks for Mac and a set of programs in the MYOB series.

See Chapters 9 and 10 for a feel for the applications that come preinstalled on your Mac mini and those available from other software publishers.

How do I keep my software current?

Keeping your software up-to-date, especially with security fixes, is very important. While Mac OS X isn't the hacker target Windows has become, it's still a good idea to make sure you have all the latest security updates installed on your machine. Fortunately, Apple makes this almost brainlessly simple to accomplish.

One of the things Apple does better than Microsoft is make updating your software easy. Despite continued requests from customers, Microsoft has been unable to create a single automatic download service for all its updates. Operating system and security fixes from Microsoft download automatically, while application updates have to be sought out and downloaded manually.

In the Macintosh world, all updates to Apple-branded software arrive automatically, so long as you have Software Update set to automatically check for new software. Mine is set to check daily, but you can also select weekly or monthly.

Of course, many Mac users are also running Microsoft Office, which is not upgraded through the Apple Software Update service. Instead, Microsoft has its own software that automatically checks for updates.

You might also be interested in a commercial service called Version-Tracker that can watch over all the software on your Mac. VersionTracker tells you when updates are available and even helps you download and install them. For information and pricing, visit www.versiontracker.com. If you have .Mac, check whether VersionTracker is still being offered for free as a part of the membership.

Are Mac magazine software reviews useful?

The Mac magazines can all be criticized, at least occasionally, for taking their role as platform cheerleader a bit too far, occasionally giving products a higher rating than they deserve. This halo effect can be a bit troubling at times, but fortunately most Mac software is available on a "try before you buy" free download basis.

There is some very wonderful Mac software available, but not all programs are wonderful just because they run on a Mac. But magazines have pages to fill, so some products get boosted that probably shouldn't be.

3

Which Mac mini to Buy (and Where to Buy It)

This chapter is primarily for readers who have not yet purchased a Mac mini. Yes, there are only two models to choose from, but there are still a handful of choices to make about specific components you should buy.

As you read this chapter, you will learn:

- How to select the Mac mini that's right for you.

- The best place to buy a Mac mini.

In the next few pages, I describe the two Mac mini models and all the options available from Apple to help you decide what's best for your needs.

Which Mac mini you purchase should reflect your needs balanced against your circumstances. My recommendation is to buy as much Mac mini as you can afford. You can add accessories later, but making changes to the basic system should be avoided.

The only easily user-upgradeable part in your Mac mini is the memory. The Mac mini has a single slot, and when you upgrade, you must remove the old memory. This will leave you with a 256 MB or—worse—a 512 MB memory module that you can't use and eBay may not want. You can add a USB Bluetooth device later, but it will use a precious USB port. Self-installation of the AirPort Extreme card, easily accomplished in other Macs, is not recommended in the cramped confines of the Mac mini.

Which Mac mini for You?

As I write this, Apple offers the Mac mini in two models:

- 1.25 GHz PowerPC G4 processor, 40 GB hard drive, $499

- 1.42 GHz PowerPC G4 processor, 80 GB hard drive, $599

Both models come with 256 MB of RAM.

At first, I was reluctant to recommend the $499 model to anyone, but I just checked and found that my still-quite-usable PowerBook G4 Titanium has only a 667 MHz processor and a 30 GB 4200 RPM hard drive. Compared to the TiBook, as the model was called, the low-end Mac mini measures up quite well—except in one area: The TiBook has 512 MB of RAM, which I consider the minimum amount of memory any Macintosh should have—including the Mac mini.

Still, developers are always demanding higher performance, and the $599 Mac mini delivers. The difference in processor speed was quite noticeable in testing done by *MacAddict* magazine. Also, the larger hard drive will come in handy if you want to build a music library, digital photo collection, or both.

And if you have any interest in editing home movies on the Mac mini, you'll need all the speed and drive space you can get.

As for memory, *MacAddict* tested its Mac minis with an extra 256 MB installed, bringing the machine up to a respectable 512 MB of RAM. I don't know of any serious Mac user—regardless of model—who is running with only 256 MB.

My recommendation: If you can afford the extra $100, buy the $599 model. I also recommend adding 256 MB of memory, for a total of 512 MB. That will add $75 to the bill. If I could only afford $599, I'd still buy that model and add the memory later.

 If Apple changes the technical specs of the Mac mini, perhaps by bumping the processor to a higher speed or releasing new models, I will post an updated recommendation at this book's Web site: www.peachpit.com/coursey.

How much memory?

A stock Mac mini comes with 256 MB of memory. Yes, the machine will run on that amount, but it won't run well, and you will be limited in the number of applications that you can have open simultaneously. This is a bigger issue than most people realize since people often have e-mail, instant messaging, iTunes, and other programs running in the background, where they aren't seen but still use processor cycles.

Adding another 256 MB of RAM improves the situation greatly. Apple charges $75 for the upgrade, which involves removing the 256 MB module that comes with the Mac mini and replacing it with a 512 MB module.

If you buy your Mac mini with the standard 256 MB and later decide to add new memory, you can take your Mac mini to an Apple Store or ship your machine in for service. Or you can perform the upgrade yourself, provided you're willing to use two thin-bladed paint scrapers to open the case (possibly voiding your warranty as well as damaging the case). I strongly recommend avoiding all of these upgrade-later scenarios, however, and just buying enough memory in the first place. (If you must do it yourself, you can Google the instructions for opening a Mac mini, but I won't take responsibility for what you do to your computer with the paint scrapers, okay?)

Apple also offers a 1 GB memory upgrade, currently $325. While I am sure a "gig" of memory would improve overall performance, it also makes the Mac mini too expensive for many would-be owners. If you think you need this much memory, you can buy it from a non-Apple source and either install it yourself or pay someone else to install it for you.

My recommendation: Purchase your Mac mini with an extra 256 MB of memory, for 512 MB total. This amount—512 MB—is fine, and 1 GB seems like overkill to me.

Which optical drive?

The stock drive in the Mac mini is what Apple calls a Combo drive. This drive lets you play DVDs and play or record CDs. For $100, you can upgrade to a SuperDrive, which allows you to write DVDs and CDs as well as read them. If you want to create home videos that can be shown on consumer DVD players, you need this upgrade.

You might also want the SuperDrive because it allows you to back up data onto a DVD disc—handy considering that each disc can hold about 4.4 GB of data. This is how I keep a copy of all my iTunes music and digital photographs, using the Backup software you can download as part of a .Mac membership.

You can also back up to an external hard drive or even an iPod if you like. I carry some of my most important files around on a 20 GB iPod as well as a 1 GB iPod shuffle.

My recommendation: Get the SuperDrive. It makes DVDs of your home movies and provides data insurance—what's not to like? (But the insurance exists only if you actually use the drive to back up your data. Refer to Chapter 7 for more information on protecting your Mac mini.)

How will you connect?

The Mac mini includes a 56K v.92 dial-up modem and an Ethernet port. The modem is used for a dial-up Internet connection, and the Ethernet port can link the Mac mini to a wired network or a cable or DSL broadband modem.

These are all fine if you want to connect only one computer at a time to the Internet and the Mac mini is located near a telephone outlet for dial-up/DSL access or a cable outlet for a cable modem.

In Chapter 5, I explain in detail why you should set up a wireless network built around an Apple AirPort Extreme Base Station. But to do that, you'll want to buy your Mac mini with an AirPort Extreme wireless card installed. This card is compatible with almost all 802.11b, 802.11g, and Wi-Fi networks. (I say "almost" because journalistic caution keeps me from saying "all," even though I have not run into network incompatibility in several years.)

The AirPort Extreme card adds $79 to the cost of the Mac mini. Unless you are sure you'll never have a wireless network, this is an upgrade I recommend.

Another wireless option is Bluetooth, used to connect the Mac mini to the Apple wireless keyboard and mouse as well as to some cellular telephones and other devices. Bluetooth adds $50, but a combined AirPort Extreme/Bluetooth package is $99. The Apple wireless keyboard and mouse combo costs $99.

If you aren't buying the AirPort Extreme card and don't have a very specific reason, I'd skip Bluetooth as well. If, however, you're following my recommendation and buying the AirPort card, then $20 for Bluetooth seems fair enough. One of these days, Bluetooth will actually do useful things, and for a mere $20 you'll be ready. Such a deal.

My recommendation: If you know you'll never have a wireless network, save your money. If you think you might go wireless someday, buy the AirPort Extreme card. If you might also want Bluetooth, buy it along with the AirPort Extreme card.

Need a keyboard and mouse?

The official reason Apple gives for not including a keyboard and mouse with the Mac mini is to allow you to use input and pointing devices you already own. That it happens to save everyone money is good news for both Apple and the customer.

The happiest situation is for a Mac mini purchaser to already own a USB mouse and keyboard. Less good, but acceptable, are devices with PS/2 connectors, which is what most people already own.

This book has an entire chapter about keyboards, displays, and mice and how you can share them between a Mac mini and one or more Windows PCs. If you are sharing, I don't recommend an Apple mouse, which has only one button instead of the two or three more common on today's PC mice.

 Know how sometimes you have to live with your mistakes? Or stubbornly refuse to admit a mistake even exists? The one-button Apple mouse is an example of this. Invented before the concept of rightclicking a two-button mouse was widely implemented in software, the Apple mouse was supposed to be easier to use. Maybe it was at one time, but it's a big limitation today, but Apple won't change. More on mice in Chapter 4.

My recommendation: Don't buy a keyboard or mouse from Apple right away. Make sure, however, that you either own a USB mouse and keyboard or purchase a PS/2-to-USB adapter so your PS/2 mouse and keyboard can be connected to the Mac mini. And read Chapter 4.

 The key placement on Mac and Windows keyboards is very slightly different, related to the placement of the Alt, Ctrl, and Windows or Command keys next to the spacebar. How to deal with this is explained in Chapter 4.

Buy a new display?

If you don't already have a display you want to use, I don't know why you'd be buying a Mac mini. The same chapter that talks about sharing a keyboard and mouse (Chapter 4) also talks about displays. The Mac mini is quite ecumenical in the displays it supports, which range from standard VGA computer monitors to some of the latest HDTV displays.

My recommendation: Use whatever display you already own and replace it when you feel the need.

Need an extended warranty?

I generally consider extended warranties a bad deal. That doesn't mean I haven't bought one—but only one, and it was for an expensive

Dell machine. The cost of the Dell plan, however, wasn't nearly as large a percentage of the cost of the hardware it protects as what Apple wants for its extended warranty.

For $149, AppleCare extends the basic 90-day software/1-year hardware warranty to 3 years for both. The extended warranty also covers your Apple-branded software and operating system. In independent surveys, Apple gets good marks for the support it provides.

Still, we're talking about a $149 extended warranty for a computer that, depending on how it's equipped, costs anywhere from $499 to $1,100. I have a hard time recommending a $149 warranty on a $499 computer. However, if you need hand-holding, Apple is happy to provide it at a price that is a lot less than what you would pay on a per-hour or per-call basis.

My recommendation: Apple hardware is well constructed, and if it doesn't blow up in the first year, it will probably make it three years. But if you are uncomfortable with computers or just feel you need access to extended support, don't let me talk you out of it. This is your call.

Also see what I have to say about Apple ProCare in the discussion of Apple's retail stores, later in this chapter.

Where to Buy Your Mac mini

There are several ways to purchase a Mac mini. Which is "easiest" depends on what matters to you. So I'll outline four ways to purchase your new computer and present the pros and cons of each.

Apple's retail stores

An Apple Store, if one is close to you, is the best place to buy a Mac mini (go to www.apple.com/retail/ to find a store close to you). Prices at the Apple Stores are the same whether you shop in person or online. In some cases, one or the other offers better product availability.

Yes, you can get a slightly better price from the online stores, but as someone new to Macintosh, you should visit an Apple Store anyway, so why not buy there? The Apple Stores sell a variety of Mac applications and accessories, as well as a few books and magazines.

If you are buying non-Apple–branded merchandise, you may find a better price at another retailer, though you may not be sure the product will work with your Mac. Most everything does, but some printers don't have Mac drivers available. The Apple Stores also carry accessories that color coordinate with your new Mac, if that matters. And you will find a selection of cables.

If you can't find what you're looking for—I am especially thinking of cables and accessories—be sure to ask. The space given to these items in most Apple Stores is small, and they are easy to overlook. Also, the stores often have these in their back rooms. If you don't ask, you may leave unnecessarily empty-handed.

Everyone who owns a computer—and especially those who don't—should visit an Apple Store. This is the only place where consumers can see demonstrations of the applications that make home computing fun, regardless of operating system.

One of the best and most popular features of the Apple retail stores is the Genius Bar, where customers used to be able to get walk-up tech support. Now it's best to make an appointment or take a number and come back at the appointed time. What Apple really wants is for you to spend $99 for its ProCare support, which is separate from the $149 extended warranty. ProCare customers get priority access to the Genius Bar. If this bugs you a bit, it probably should.

The Apple retail stores accept all Apple hardware for repair, regardless of where it was purchased.

Another retail store

Before there were Apple Stores, there were stores that sold Apple computers. Those are almost all gone now, and Macs have become pretty hard to find outside of the Apple-owned retail stores. This is sad, but it's also how business works. Those stores that still exist seem to get merchandise some time after it appears in Apple's own stores. Imagine that.

I am all for supporting small merchants, but Apple has made it very clear where we're supposed to buy our Macs.

Apple's online store

The Apple online store (store.apple.com/) offers a larger selection of products than the retail locations. It is also a good place to find cables and adapters and other add-ons, especially iPod goodies. I have been pleased with the online store's service, but I also pass as many as four Apple Stores when I drive into San Francisco, so I usually shop in person.

tip   You can always visit the Apple's online store to see what's available and then compare prices at other online merchants. Sometimes I've noticed that Apple doesn't provide enough information, such as model numbers, to make this possible.

Another online store

There are several Mac specialty merchants online. Their prices are usually very close to what Apple charges, but they generally include special deals with hardware purchases. Buy your Mac mini from one of these online stores, and you may get a "free" printer or something else you may or may not need. The major online Mac stores, such as Mac Mall and MacConnection, are reputable and may be able to fill your order more quickly than Apple's online store.

My recommendation: Buy your Mac mini directly from Apple unless you really need the free printer or whatever the online merchants are offering this week. I don't think other vendors offer enough added value to recommend them for Apple-branded items. However, for non-Apple merchandise, the Apple specialists should be able to assure you of compatibility with your Mac mini.

tip   You won't find all things Mac in the Apple Stores. Check out the magazines, especially *Macworld* (www.macworld.com), *MacDirectory* (www.macdirectory.com), and *MacAddict* (www.macaddict.com), for reviews, buying advice, and advertising.

4

Sharing Your Display, Keyboard, and Mouse

Certainly, many buyers of the Mac mini switching from a Windows machine will just unplug their PCs and put them in the closet. Others, however, will want to keep their PCs around so they can continue to use Windows-only applications or make full use of a Microsoft Exchange server. This chapter is for those latter users, who aren't so much switchers as adders.

As you read this chapter, you will learn:

- How to share a single display, keyboard, and mouse between a Mac mini and a Windows PC.

- How to select the necessary keyboard-video-mouse (KVM) switch.

- How to deal with a lack of USB and FireWire ports on the Mac mini.

- How to select USB and FireWire hubs to expand your Mac mini.

- About the important difference between Mac and Windows keyboards and how to deal with it.

- How to select speakers to use with your Mac mini.

- How to share data between your Mac mini and a Windows PC.

It is easy for your Mac mini and Windows PC to share the same display, keyboard, and mouse. All that's required is a single piece of additional equipment: a KVM switch, costing as little as $60. If there is one essential accessory for the Mac mini, this is it.

The letters *KVM* stand for keyboard, video, and mouse, all of which the device switches between the two computers. Press the switch one way, and you'll see your Mac mini's desktop on the display; press it the other way, and your PC's Windows desktop appears. Whichever computer appears on the screen is also the machine to which your keyboard and mouse are connected.

Some KVM switches also switch your speakers along with your keyboard, display, and mouse. And the one I'm using now doesn't even require pressing a switch—just four keystrokes, and my screen changes from one machine to the other. And the actual switch is hidden under my desk.

Buying a KVM Switch

KVM switches come in two flavors based on the connectors they use: USB and PS/2. Choosing the right one—along with any required cables and adapters—may save you money and definitely will save you a run back to the computer store. You may still prefer to buy a new keyboard and mouse.

Here's the problem: Most Windows PCs come with a PS/2-style keyboard and mouse. The name PS/2 comes from the IBM PC model on which this connector first appeared. You will recognize PS/2 connectors by their colors. The keyboard connector is purple and the mouse connector is green (**Figure 4.1**). They typically plug into connectors of the same color on the back of the Windows computer, often near the top.

Figure 4.1

These are PS/2 connectors from a KVM switch. The purple connector (second from the right) is at the end of a keyboard cable. The green connector (far right) is at the end of a mouse cable. On the far left is the display connector; second from the left is the audio connector.

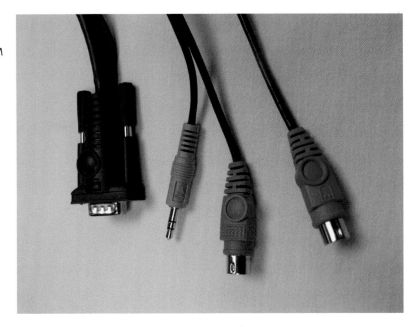

The Mac mini, however, lacks PS/2 connectors and expects its keyboard and mouse to come equipped with USB connectors (**Figure 4.2**). PCs also have USB connectors, but I am not sure that any PC manufacturer routinely ships a USB keyboard and mouse with its products.

Figure 4.2

The USB connector at the end of a USB mouse cable.

If you want to continue using a PS/2 mouse and keyboard, you should buy a PS/2-equipped KVM switch and a PS/2-to-USB adapter for your Mac mini. The adapter connects the separate PS/2 mouse and keyboard cables to a single USB port on the Mac mini.

Maybe, however, you have replaced the original mouse and keyboard that came with your PC. In that case, you may now have USB connectors on your mouse and keyboard as well as your Mac mini and PC. This is a happy situation because it saves you from buying an adaptor on the Mac mini side.

If you are using a USB keyboard and mouse, you should buy a USB-equipped KVM switch. If you happen to be shopping for a new keyboard and mouse, most of what is available today is USB.

You can buy KVM switches capable of switching between more than two computers. The one I usually use can switch among four machines. But for simplicity, this chapter will discuss only two-port switches.

The good news is that actually connecting and using a KVM switch with your Mac mini and a PC is easier than deciding which switch to buy, and setup should take less time than reading this chapter. All we're really doing is making nine connections: three to each machine plus the display, keyboard, and mouse.

tip

Before buying anything, make a list of what you need and the prices associated with each option. The list will include the KVM switch (all you need if you have a USB keyboard and mouse and buy a USB KVM switch). But if you have a PS/2 keyboard and mouse, you should compare the cost of replacing them with USB models with the cost of buying a PS/2-to-USB adapter for the Mac mini. Also, USB and PS/2 KVM switches may vary in price.

My recommendation: Replace your PS/2 mouse and keyboard with USB models. I am not a big fan of connecting a wireless keyboard and mouse to a KVM switch because it adds another point of failure, but it can be done.

tip

Don't forget that if your KVM switch doesn't have built-in cables or come prepackaged with them, you'll have to buy a cable assembly for each computer you want to connect to the KVM switch. This can get expensive.

VGA vs. DVI

What I am about to say will apply to very few of you.

Some PC makers are starting to equip some of their machines with DVI digital video outputs, just like what Apple provides with the Mac mini. Some computer displays and a larger number of home theater–style monitors have DVI inputs.

DVI is used to send digital video from one device to another. VGA is analog and, in theory, of lower quality than DVI.

If you have DVI capabilities on your PC and monitor, then you are a candidate for a DVI-based KVM switch. These have only recently started to be widely available, though not so widely that you might not have trouble finding one.

If you are connecting a stand-alone Mac mini to your home entertainment system and DVI is an option, by all means use it.

If you are connecting a Mac mini and a PC to the same display, I recommend the standard VGA connection, if only because DVI cables and KVM switches are more expensive.

The Mac mini comes equipped with a DVI-to-VGA connector that allows a standard PC monitor cable to connect to the Mac mini.

Which KVM switch to buy?

KVM switches used to be quite expensive. I remember paying more than $200 for my first one, plus $40 per connected computer for cables. The switch itself was a decent-sized box that sat next to the computer and had push buttons for selecting the computer to be connected to the keyboard, video, and mouse.

Fortunately, prices have come down, and the switches themselves have become smaller, easier to use, and decidedly more stylish. And some

KVM switches now have the ability to switch audio and even USB peripherals as well.

Over the years, I have played with many KVM switches, including the Belkin models that Apple sells in its retail stores and online. These work nicely, but are large when compared to the Mac mini itself. The Belkin SOHO USB 2-port KVM switch includes cables and sells for $129.

I have also used the IOGEAR KVM switches that are equipped with built-in cables and sell for less than $80. What I like about these is that there are no switches to push—just press the Ctrl, Shift, and Alt keys, in that order, and reasonably quickly the keyboard's Caps Lock and Scroll Lock lights alternately flash. That's my cue to press the 1 key to select the Mac mini or the 2 key to select the PC. It takes a lot less time to switch machines with the IOGEAR KVM switch than it takes to explain how to do it.

IOGEAR is my favorite brand of KVM switch, specifically the models with no switches and cables attached. But I have nothing bad to say about Belkin, which makes a wide range of fine Mac accessories. Buy what makes sense to you.

Visit www.iogear.com and www.belkin.com and see what each company has to offer. Each company regularly brings out new models.

IOGEAR uses an all-in-one design in which the six-foot output cables are permanently attached to the switch. This is very convenient, although it limits the distance that the computers and the display/keyboard/mouse can be separated. There are no buttons on the switch, allowing it to be dropped behind a desk or wherever you want to hide it (**Figure 4.3**).

The IOGEAR switch is designed to work with a USB keyboard and USB mouse. While you connect the keyboard and mouse to separate ports on the KVM switch, they are combined and require only a single USB port on the Mac and PC. This is important for the Mac mini, which has only two built-in USB ports.

Figure 4.3

This is the IOGEAR USB KVM switch that I used while writing most of this book. It lived under my desk. It has built-in cables, supports audio, and uses keystrokes for switching.

No special software is required on either Mac or PC.

The IOGEAR switch is self-powered, eliminating the need for yet another "wall-wart" power supply. It has USB sniffing technology for USB mouse and keyboard emulation to ensure smooth startups, as well as support for Plug-n-Play monitors and most wheel mice. IOGEAR says its patented VSE Video Signal Enhancement technology provides 32-bit color at resolutions up to 2048 x 1536 pixels.

The Belkin SOHO Series USB KVM switch offers more features than the IOGEAR, but also costs more and requires space on your desk (**Figure 4.4**). Belkin offers both audio and microphone support, enabling you to switch between speakers and microphones without having to reconnect.

Also included with the Belkin switch is a two-port USB hub, allowing peripherals to be switched between the two computers. This is a neat feature for people with printers and Web cams and other devices that they want to use with both computers.

Figure 4.4
This is a Belkin PS/2-style KVM switch. Cables are included, and it uses a button for switching.

tip Here's what I am recommending to friends: IOGEAR Miniview Micro USB Plus KVM (model GCS632U). This is a two-port KVM switch that has been tested by Apple to ensure compatibility with the Mac mini as well as with Windows PCs. Besides the usual keyboard, video, and mouse switching support common to all KVM switches, this switch is capable of switching audio between two computers and a single set of speakers.

Connecting Your KVM Switch

Here's what you will need to connect your KVM switch:

- Mac mini computer
- The DVI-to-VGA adapter included with your Mac mini
- Windows PC computer
- Display
- Keyboard
- Mouse
- KVM switch
- Any KVM cables that may be required
- PS/2-to-USB adapter, if required (**Figure 4.5**)

Figure 4.5

A PS/2-to-USB adapter, used to connect a PS/2 KVM switch to a Mac mini.

When you've gathered these items, you are ready to begin.

Important: Your PC should already be up and running with the display, keyboard, and mouse you plan to share between the two computers. If your PC isn't working, solve *that* problem before proceeding.

Ideally, your Mac mini is still in the box. But if you've already booted it up, that's okay, too, though it means you're already connected to something.

Here's the step-by-step plan:

1. Power down everything. This includes the PC and display. To be safe, you should unplug these from the wall, though it's not absolutely necessary.

2. Disconnect the monitor, mouse, and keyboard from the back of the PC.

3. Open the KVM package. Some KVM switches require external power; some don't.

4. Connect the display, keyboard, and mouse to the KVM switch, assuming that your switch matches to connectors on your mouse

and keyboard: PS/2 or USB. If the connectors don't match, reread the earlier part of this chapter and go buy the right adapters. If you bought a USB KVM switch by mistake, you're probably better off buying a new USB mouse and keyboard.

5. Connect the display, keyboard, and mouse cables from the KVM switch to your Windows PC.

6. Read the KVM switch directions to make sure you know how the switch operates. You may use a push button or a keyboard command to switch between the two computers.

7. Open the Mac mini and remove it from the box. Do not connect it to a power source, but do connect the included DVI-to-VGA adapter (a white piece of plastic that has connectors on both ends) to the DVI video output on the Mac mini (**Figure 4.6**).

8. Connect the monitor cable from the KVM switch to the Mac mini. Also connect the keyboard and mouse cables. This assumes that you have the PS/2 keyboard and mouse adapter, if required. Do not connect power to the Mac mini.

9. Reconnect the power to the PC and monitor. Power up the PC.

Figure 4.6
Do not lose this piece, or you won't be connecting a PC monitor to your Mac mini. This is the VGA-to-DVI adapter that is packed with the Mac mini.

10. Set the KVM switch to connect the PC to your display, keyboard, and mouse. Watch the PC start up, and make sure the display, keyboard, and mouse are functioning correctly. If they aren't, you've connected something improperly.

11. When the PC is working properly, connect the power supply to the Mac mini.

12. Power up the Mac mini and select it on the KVM switch. Watch the Mac mini start, and make sure the display, keyboard, and mouse are functioning correctly. If they aren't, you've connected something improperly.

You can now switch back and forth between your Mac mini and PC. See how easy that was?

About Hubs

The one thing I don't like about the Mac mini, besides having to buy more memory, is the shortage of USB and FireWire ports. The Mac mini has two USB 2.0 ports and one FireWire 400 port (**Figure 4.7**). That is barely enough for some users and clearly not enough for others.

Figure 4.7
Most PC users know what a USB connector looks like (it's on the right) but are less familiar with a FireWire connector (on the left), widely used to connect video cameras, iPods, and other devices to Macintosh computers.

Which will you be?

In a minimalist installation, you will use one of the two USB ports for your keyboard and mouse (combined into one port by your KVM or PS/2-to-USB adapter). The single FireWire port will be available for an iPod, iSight camera, video camera, or external FireWire hard drive or other peripheral.

You might use the extra USB port for connecting a printer, iPod shuffle, digital still camera, or pen input device, such as a Wacom tablet.

Many people will want to connect several devices at once and will find the Mac mini's limited number of ports to be a problem. Fortunately, there are devices, called hubs, that can increase the number of available ports. They are easy to buy and not terribly expensive.

Reminder: USB and FireWire ports are different types of connections and are not interchangeable. That means adding both USB and FireWire hubs if you need both. And make sure the hubs you buy support USB 2.0 and FireWire 400, lest you end up with an older and slower, though less expensive, hub.

You can buy a KVM switch from Belkin that also includes a two-port USB hub that switches between computers when you switch the keyboard, display, and mouse. This seems particularly useful if you want to share a USB printer or maybe a camera between your Mac mini and a PC.

In writing this book, I've used both Belkin USB and FireWire hubs and a combined USB-FireWire hub from IOMEGA.

A Tale of Two Keyboards

One the great things about the Mac mini is that it works with any USB keyboard. One of the bad things about USB keyboards is that Apple and Windows keyboards are slightly different. This can cause confusion when you're moving back and forth between Mac OS X and Windows.

Windows keyboards don't have the Command (sometimes also called Apple) and Option keys familiar to Mac users. In their places, on both sides of the spacebar, are the Alt and Windows keys. The keys do more or less the same things on their respective systems. The Apple and

Windows keys do pretty much the same thing, although the Apple key sometimes takes the role that Windows assigns to the Ctrl key. The Windows Alt and Mac Option keys are also generally equivalent.

The problem is that these keys are laid out opposite between the two operating systems. When you use a Windows keyboard with a Mac mini (or any Mac), the Command and Option keys are switched.

This is the sequence on a Windows keyboard:

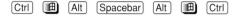

This is the sequence on a Mac keyboard:

[Ctrl] [Option] [Cmd] [Spacebar] [Cmd] [Option] [Ctrl]

This difference is, to a large extent, more confusing to describe than it is to live with. But I tend not to use keyboard shortcuts. For those people who do use shortcuts, key placement is more of an issue.

Fortunately, what is done in software can be changed in software. And there is a utility program for Mac OS X that's specifically designed to bring your rowdy keyboard under control.

DoubleCommand (doublecommand.sourceforge.net/) is a free program that lets you swap the functionality of the Windows and Alt keys, making your Windows keyboard work just like a Mac keyboard. It can make other keyboard changes as well, but this simple swap is what will make Windows users feel right at home on their new Mac minis.

tip   **I have gotten so adjusted to pressing the different keys when I switch from Mac to Windows that I don't even bother with DoubleCommand. But I am a hunt-and-peck typist, and a touch typist might feel differently. Play around and see what works best for you.**

An alternative is to use a KVM switch just for video and use separate keyboards and pointing devices for each of your machines. For example, if your Mac mini has the built-in Bluetooth wireless option, you can use the Apple wireless keyboard and mouse. I've done this on occasion, and it allows the Mac mini's keyboard and mouse to be easily stored when not in use.

One reason to use separate keyboards, even if it means running a cable from each keyboard to its respective computer, is so you can continue using the special features on some PC keyboards. This functionality is often lost when such a keyboard is used with a KVM switch.

The Apple Bluetooth wireless keyboard and mouse option is especially valuable in home entertainment applications because it allows you to sit some distance away from the computer and monitor. This can be important from convenience, aesthetic, and safety standpoints.

If you do end up using a wired Apple keyboard and mouse with your Mac mini, you save a USB port because the mouse plugs into one of the two USB ports on the keyboard itself.

While I'd hate to have to physically swap screens when I move from the Mac mini to Windows and back, I sometimes don't mind having two keyboards and mice connected to two separate machines.

Speakers

Your Mac mini has a dual speaker/line-out jack on the rear panel. If you have a KVM switch with audio capabilities, you can plug it into the jack. This is usually a light green connector (see Figure 4.1). The benefit of this is that you can hear both the Mac mini and PC through a single pair of speakers. The downside is that you can listen to only one computer at a time.

I prefer to have separate speakers on my Mac mini and my PC, allowing me to use one for music or Internet radio while working on the other. That's what I recommend, though it does require two sets of speakers.

If you want to feed music from your Mac mini to speakers in other rooms, check out the discussion of the Apple AirPort Express wireless device in Chapter 5.

As for what speakers to choose, this is one place where I recommend getting the best you can afford, so listen around. You don't have to spend a fortune to get good-sounding audio. Your ears (and music collection) are a terrible thing to waste on rotten sound.

5

Connecting Your Mac mini to the Internet

Connecting your Mac mini to the Internet can be a snap, and setting up a home network isn't much more trouble. Apple makes it easy to get online. And with an AirPort Express Base Station, you can stream music from the iTunes library on your Mac mini to your home stereo.

As you read this chapter, you will learn:

- How to connect your Mac mini to the Internet.

- How to share a wired or wireless Internet connection among your Mac mini and some number of Windows computers.

- How to set up a wireless network.

- Why an Apple wireless base station may be your best buy.

- The wonders of the AirPort Express Base Station.

Dear Reader:

As I begin this chapter, I wish you could be sitting here with me so that I could ask you questions. You'd tell me what you already have for an Internet connection, and I'd tell you how to share that connection among your Mac mini and however many Windows computers you own.

We'd decide whether a wireless network makes sense for you, or whether a wired network will do the job. If you already have a wireless network, we'd discuss replacing your current base station with an Apple AirPort Extreme to get some special features, such as the ability to send iTunes music around your home and to share printers easily with your Windows computers and your Mac mini.

If I knew your answers, I could write a networking chapter especially for you, written precisely to your level of experience and including only things you need to know. I'd have your Mac mini and Windows PC both connected to the Internet, one way or another, in no time flat.

Sadly, you're not sitting on my couch, and I can't ask you questions. So this chapter is longer and more complex than necessary to meet just your particular needs. I must meet as many people's needs as possible, and this makes some complexity inevitable.

The good news is that networking information can be divided according to broad categories of users, so that is how I will present it. I've organized the chapter into common scenarios, allowing you to select one that closely matches your situation and what you'd like to accomplish.

tip

Macintosh networking is simple. Looking at this chapter doesn't make it seem that way, but getting a Macintosh connected to the Internet is usually pretty easy. In that spirit, read "Connecting Your Mac mini to the Internet" in Chapter 2 before continuing here if you run into problems or just want to know more about connecting a Mac mini and Windows PC to the same Internet connection.

Connecting Your Mac mini to Your Internet Connection

When you first turn on your Mac mini, the setup software will do its best to get you connected to the Internet, provided you have the proper cable plugged into the Mac mini.

You have a single PC connected to the Internet and want to share that connection with your Mac mini

To connect your Mac mini to the Internet using the same connection as your PC, simply remove the cable that connects your PC to the Internet and insert it in the proper connector on the rear panel of your Mac mini.

If you use a dial-up Internet connection with your PC: Gather the required telephone number, user name, and password. Unplug the modem cable from your PC and plug it into the modem jack on your Mac mini.

If you use a DSL or cable modem with your PC: Gather the user name and password (if required). Unplug the Ethernet cable from your PC and plug it into the Ethernet port on the Mac mini.

Now turn on your Mac mini.

Follow the on-screen instructions during setup, and you will quickly be connected to the Internet.

Just one problem: You will be able to connect only one computer at a time to the Internet. And you must change the cable whenever you want to change which computer is connected to the Internet. Maybe this won't bother you, or perhaps you will decide that having only one computer connected to the Internet is just fine. Then you don't have to worry about changing cables.

If you go this route, I recommend that you use the Mac mini as your Internet computer. The Mac mini comes with excellent Internet software, and Mac OS X is a significantly more secure operating system than Microsoft Windows XP. (See Chapter 7 for a security discussion.)

You have a home network and want to connect your Mac mini to it

If you already have a network, you can connect your Mac mini to it at any time, as your Mac mini should recognize the Internet connection whenever you use or change it. The default network settings on the Mac mini are usually fine, so:

If you have a wired home network, connect an Ethernet cable from the port on the back of the Mac mini to your Ethernet hub or access point (wherever the PC is connected). Your Mac mini and Windows computer(s) should be sharing an Internet connection when the Mac mini's setup process is completed, if you make the connection before you first launch your Mac mini, or as quickly as your already established Mac mini recognizes the new connection, which usually happens automatically.

If you have a wireless home network, the procedure is a little more complex, but only because the Mac mini setup process may not recognize your wireless network, or your Mac mini's AirPort Extreme card may not be turned on. However, these issues are easily remedied once setup is complete.

Figure 5.1
The AirPort icon appears in the menu bar at the top of your Mac mini's screen. The number of curved lines indicates signal strength, here shown at maximum.

If the automatic network installation during initial setup does not connect your Mac mini to your existing home wireless network, click the AirPort icon in the menu bar and turn on the AirPort Extreme wireless card inside the Mac mini (**Figures 5.1** and **5.2**). You then select the name of wireless network you want to join and enter the network password. Mac OS X can save your network preferences, including the password, and automatically connect whenever you start your Mac mini.

Figure 5.2

Click and hold the AirPort icon, and a menu similar to this will pop down. This is the easiest place to turn your AirPort Extreme card on and off and to select the network you wish to join.

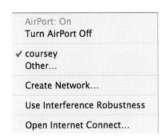

All network setup is usually pretty easy on any Mac, and this is equally true for the Mac mini. Follow the setup instructions and help screens, and you should have no trouble getting connected.

tip

If the default settings do not succeed, it is likely because your existing network has been set up manually (with a fixed IP address, for example). In this case, whoever set up your network should be able to provide you with the proper settings, which you should enter in the Mac mini's System Preferences Network pane. The Mac mini's internal firewall and file sharing are controlled by the Sharing System Preferences pane. AirPort base stations are configured using the AirPort Setup Assistant or the AirPort Admin Utility. You will find these in the Utilities folder, in the Applications folder, on your Mac mini's hard drive.

Most of the time, network setup on a Mac is automatic. But if you need to enter a phone number or password for a dial-up connection, you may need to open the Internet Connect application, in your Applications folder. **Figures 5.3**, **5.4**, and **5.5** show Internet Connect in action.

Figure 5.3

This is the icon for Internet Connect, in the Applications folder. If you're using the Mac mini's built-in modem to connect to the Internet, start here. Internet Connect is not used for AOL nor the introductory EarthLink account in the Utilities folder.

Figure 5.4
Here is where you use Internet Connect to set up the Mac mini to use its built-in modem to dial an Internet service provider.

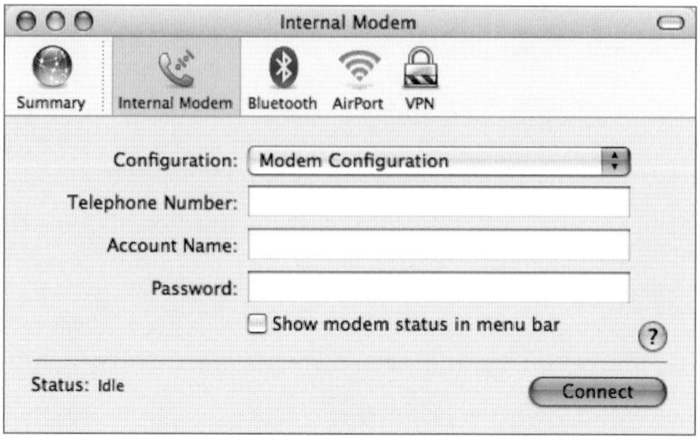

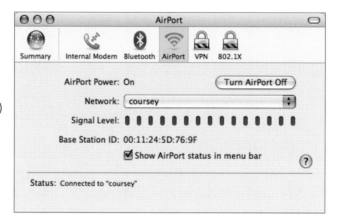

Figure 5.5
Internet Connect can also be used to set up an AirPort connection (if your Mac mini is equipped with the AirPort Extreme option) as well as a VPN connection to the network at your office.

If you get really stuck, use your Windows machine to view the support information on Apple.com, visit the Genius Bar at your local Apple Store, contact Apple tech support, or drop me a line at coursey@mac.com and I will do my best to help you.

tip   If you already own a wireless network, but it's running the older and slower Wi-Fi 802.11b technology, getting a Mac mini is an excellent reason to upgrade your entire network. You can do this all at once and replace all the existing cards on your Windows machines, or you can just replace your current base station with the AirPort Extreme. More on this later in the chapter.

Connecting When You Don't Have a Home Network—But Want One

If you want to simultaneously connect your Mac mini and one or more Windows PCs to a high-speed, broadband Internet connection, you need a network.

The easiest to create and most flexible networks use Apple's AirPort Extreme hardware, which is perfectly compatible with both Macs and Windows computers, especially those running Windows XP.

In the next section, I will tell you how to build a wireless network from scratch.

About Broadband

I continue to run into people who don't understand what a broadband Internet connection is or why they might want one. Some people have good reasons for not wanting broadband—for instance, those who have a fast Internet connection at work and don't use a computer very much at home. There are also people for whom a $50-a-month broadband service is just too expensive. For everyone else, here's why you want broadband, starting with a definition of what broadband is.

There are many ways to think about broadband, most involving the actual speed of the connection it provides to the Internet. Broadband is available from cable and satellite TV companies as well as from telephone companies and the few independent broadband companies that are still in business.

Cable broadband is delivered using the same cable that brings in your cable TV signal. Satellite broadband is downlinked using your dish antenna. You may uplink to the satellite as well or use a dial-up modem to send commands and upload files. *Satellite* connections are generally a last resort for people who can't get broadband any other way, usually because they live in the sticks. There are also some microwave broadband providers. They typically attach a flat panel antenna outside the customer's home or office and connect to a central antenna located on a tall structure.

DSL is provided by local telephone companies and a few remaining independent providers. DSL is delivered over your existing dial-up telephone line and does not require a separate line. DSL uses a special modem that does not tie up your voice line. You can place and receive telephone calls while you are using your DSL connection (which is always available). Some DSL connections require you to enter a user name and password to connect. However, connection is usually handled automatically by your computer, and you will not even be aware it is taking place.

A broadband connection is (or should be) much faster than a dial-up Internet connection. The precise speeds vary, but a broadband connection typically runs at from 384 Kbps to as much as 6 Mbps. The more you pay, the faster a connection you get. Compare that with your dial-up modem, which tops out at 56 Kbps and rarely runs that fast.

Broadband is useful for sending or receiving files, downloading music or video, watching video or listening to music over the Internet, and sending digital photos as e-mail. You can also use a broadband Internet connection for long-distance voice telephone service. A company called Vonage (www.vonage.com) is a pioneer in making this "Voice over Internet Protocol," or VoIP technology, available to consumers and small businesses.

A broadband connection makes it easier to use the iDisk feature of your .Mac account as well as to download automatic updates from Apple or new software from software companies that make their products available for download. When you have a broadband connection, your instant messaging and e-mail can be left on continually, and you can listen to Internet radio or watch online TV as much as you like.

Broadband is key to using the audio and video conferencing features of iChat AV, included with your Mac mini. You can easily share a broadband connection with the other computers in your home—and even with your neighbors if you use a wireless network to connect your computers to one another.

By sharing your Internet connection with others outside your home, you may be violating your agreement with your broadband provider—some don't allow sharing a connection. Use caution and find out if sharing your connection will get you into trouble. However, many follow the old adage, "It's easier to apologize than to ask permission."

Caution: A broadband connection may be always on and connected to the Internet, which creates a potential security issue that firewalls are intended to handle—after all, a computer that's always connected to the Internet is more likely to be noticed by hackers than one that's on only when you dial up your ISP.

On the positive side, because the connection is always there, you don't have to wait to use it when you sit down at the computer. There's no waiting for your modem to dial, and no busy signals. Broadband does not require a special telephone line, so if you have a separate line for your computer, you can have it disconnected and apply the money toward your broadband connection. Cable modems, of course, require no telephone line at all.

Depending on how your DSL is connected, you may need one or more inexpensive filters attached between your telephones and wall jacks. These are usually included with the DSL modem but may be purchased separately at consumer electronics and computer stores.

Typical broadband service costs $50 a month. I consider it an excellent investment.

Creating a Wireless Network for Your Home

I love home networks and think everyone who has more than one computer should have one. The "killer application" for a home network is the ability to share a single broadband Internet connection among several computers, such as a Mac mini and one or more Windows machines.

In this section, I'll explain the basics of setting up a network that can connect both Macs and PCs to a single Internet connection. You will also be able to share printers and send your iTunes music to the stereo systems, home theater, or powered speakers around your home. And you will do this without the long cable runs otherwise necessary to connect everything together.

My ideas vs. your budget

I have some definite ideas about how a home or small business network should be built. If there will be Macs on the network, I also have definite ideas about the equipment you should buy.

My biases:

People with multiple computers in their homes should use a wireless network to connect them. But a single Mac mini and single Windows PC sitting on the same desk don't really benefit from wireless and can be connected to an Ethernet hub using cables. Having a wireless network allows people who visit your home or office to easily connect to the Internet. If they have a wireless card in their portable computer, all they need to know to connect is your network's name and password.

Apple's AirPort Express Base Stations are very handy. These support a shared USB printer, wired Ethernet connection, and wireless distribution of iTunes music to remote speakers. AirPort Express units can also extend the range of your wireless network. And they can do all these things simultaneously. Unfortunately, AirPort Express works well only with an Apple AirPort Extreme Base Station (**Figure 5.6**), and it doesn't work at all with most other base stations. So...

I've retrofitted my home network with AirPort Extreme and Express Base Stations. I did this because I liked being able to wirelessly stream music around my house and to easily share printers. A USB printer connected to an AirPort Extreme Base Station or AirPort Express Base Station works with both Mac OS X and Windows XP computers.

Figure 5.6
Apple's AirPort base station hardware is available in two models: the standard AirPort Extreme Base Station (right) and the AirPort Express Base Station (left). (Courtesy Apple Computer)

 Replacing my Microsoft wireless access point with an AirPort Extreme Base Station cost $199. I've also bought three AirPort Express Base Stations for $129 each. Updating the Windows machines to 802.11g, using USB adapters, cost $50 to $70 per machine.

Apple's AirPort wireless card (such as the one that is optionally inside your Mac mini) is fully compatible with the Wi-Fi 802.11b and g standards and will connect to *any* network that implements them. This means that if you already have a wireless network, your wireless-equipped Mac mini will connect to it. It also means that if you bring a wireless laptop home from work, it will contact to any Apple wireless hardware you may purchase.

About AirPort

AirPort is Apple's trade name for wireless networking. This can be confusing because Apple products are compatible with other wireless networking equipment, though you might not guess it from the AirPort name.

Fortunately, all wireless hardware today is pretty much compatible across the different brands and between Windows and Macintosh. I would say 100 percent compatible since I haven't run into any hardware that won't work together, but I know that if I say that, something odd will turn up.

All you need to know is this: Buy 802.11g cards for your PCs. Do not buy the older 802.11b, which will work with your network but at one-fifth the speed of your AirPort Extreme hardware. For desktop Windows machines, I recommend USB wireless adapters because they are easy to install. Notebook PCs should get a standard wireless card. Remember: Buy 802.11g cards and adapters only. I recommend paying a bit more to get a brand name you recognize.

The instructions that are included with your Windows wireless adapter or card will explain how to install the hardware. It's quite easy, but there are minor differences between brands. Installation is easier on Windows XP machines, especially those running Service Pack 2, than on other Windows computers.

More on what to buy later in this chapter.

Meet the AirPort family

At present, there are three members of the AirPort product family. They are:

AirPort Extreme Base Station (Figure 5.7). Intended to be the center of an AirPort network, this device connects to your broadband Internet connection and makes it available to the computers on your network. You can also use its built-in dial-up modem to connect to AOL and share that connection with one Macintosh at a time. I don't recommend this as your primary Internet connection, but it is convenient if you have AOL and don't want or can't get a broadband Internet connection. It is also a useful "just-in-case" backup for when your broadband fails.

Though primarily intended as a wireless base station, AirPort Extreme also has an Ethernet port that can be used with a cable (and multi-port hub if necessary) to connect computers sitting adjacent to the base station or someplace you don't mind running a cable. The wired and wireless computers will be able to talk to one another as well as the Internet.

Figure 5.7

The AirPort Extreme Base Station is the heart of the Apple wireless network. Besides providing a wireless Internet connection for wireless-equipped PCs and Macs, it has a USB port for attaching a printer that can be used by computers on the network. (Courtesy Apple Computer)

The AirPort Extreme Base Station has a USB port that can be used to share a connected USB printer with the computers on the AirPort network. The device also has a connection for an external antenna, if necessary.

AirPort Express Base Station (Figure 5.8). This is a multipurpose networking device that can be used alone or with the AirPort Extreme Base Station. The AirPort Express Base Station is a small unit that plugs directly into an electrical outlet and wirelessly connects to your AirPort Extreme Base Station. It can be used to:

- Share iTunes music around your home from either your Mac mini or a PC to a stereo, home theater, or powered speakers. You can plug a Keyspan Express remote control into the USB port and control iTunes from where you're listening. The Keyspan remote control is easy to use, but it lacks any sort of lighted keypad, making it difficult to use in a darkened room. Still, it sure beats running to the computer that's running iTunes just to change a song.

- Share a printer connected to the USB port on the AirPort Express Base Station. The shared printer can be used by both Macs and Windows XP computers and allows you to locate the printer in places where it isn't convenient to run a cable.

- Provide a wired connection to your wireless network. The AirPort Express Base Station has a built-in Ethernet port that can be connected to a computer, allowing the computer to access the network using its built-in Ethernet port and a cable connected to the base station. An 802.11g wireless adapter is much less expensive than an AirPort Express Base Station, so I'd use the base station in this way only if the base station will be located near the remote computer anyway.

- Extend the range of your network. An AirPort Express Base Station can solve the poor-signal problems that exist in some homes. Place the AirPort Express unit in an area with a good signal that's near the area where signals are a problem.

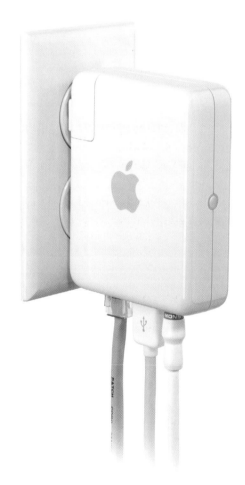

Figure 5.8

The AirPort Express Base Station plugs into a power outlet. From the bottom, you can extend an audio connection, perhaps to a home stereo; a USB connection to a printer or remote control; and an Ethernet cable that can be connected to a non-wireless-equipped computer to connect it to the Internet. This is a neat piece of hardware. (Courtesy Apple Computer)

When Apple introduced the AirPort Express Base Station, I was not sure what I would do with one, especially since it would require replacing the base station I was then using with an Apple AirPort Extreme Base Station that supported the Express's special features.

Since then, and after studying what the Express could do for me, I've installed three in my home and want one or two more. I am using them to control iTunes (from both Macs and Windows machines), to share a printer, and to extend the range of my network to an upstairs bedroom where a PC could not reliably connect to the wireless network.

AirPort Extreme cards. These are the cards that are installed inside Macintosh computers that allow them to connect to wireless networks. Although an AirPort card can be added to a Mac mini after purchase, I strongly recommend that you purchase the unit with wireless already included.

Your AirPort Extreme-equipped Mac should communicate seamlessly with any 802.11b or 802.11g hardware, no matter who makes it. Also, your 802.11b or 802.11g-equipped PCs should talk to your AirPort base station without any problems. When shopping, buy 802.11g devices.

Just to confuse us, there is another wireless LAN standard, called 802.11a. Although 802.11b (AirPort) and 802.11g (AirPort Extreme) devices can talk to each other, neither can talk with 802.11a devices. Do not buy an 802.11a device.

What is the range of an AirPort network?

The maximum claimed distance for AirPort networks is 150 feet, with speed decreasing the farther you are from the base station. There are, however, many variables, so some experimentation may be necessary. In open air on a good day, with nothing between the Mac and the access point, ranges can be several times this distance. On the other hand, inside buildings with radio-blocking materials in or on the walls, ranges may be much less.

If you have a Mac mini with built-in wireless, make certain not to set anything on the white plastic top of the unit—the wireless antenna is located just underneath the polycarbonate.

Finding the best location for your AirPort Extreme or Express Base Station may take some work. In my old house—which had three levels—I had to move the base station a few times to find a place where all the computers could talk to it. The computers must be able to talk to the base station, but they don't have to be able to talk to each other. This means that if the AirPort Extreme Base Station is in the center of the physical network, it should cover 150 feet in all directions, allowing the farthest computers to be up to 300 feet apart. The distance should be much less if you are expecting the full 54 Mbps speed the Extreme can provide.

If you use a wireless-equipped portable or have real signal problems at home, you should consider investing in a Wi-Fi finder, a small receiver that lights LEDs to indicate signal strength. Most are designed to be attached to a key ring or briefcase and cost about $30. You can use the finder to locate wireless hot spots or to determine the best signal areas in your home—or your local Starbucks.

At my new house, which has only two stories, I still have some connection problems, especially upstairs. Fortunately, the AirPort Extreme Base Station can be connected to an external antenna, sometimes capable of solving poor-signal problems. Even more fortunately, the AirPort Express Base Station can act as a wireless repeater, extending the range of the network even more.

Configuring your AirPort Extreme or AirPort Express Base Station

Both your computers and the base station must be configured before they can talk to each other and the Internet. The easiest way to do this is to plug in your AirPort Extreme Base Station and connect an Ethernet cable between your Mac mini and the base station. You can also connect wirelessly if you choose, but connecting using Ethernet cable simplifies the process.

The AirPort Setup Assistant is in the Utilities folder (**Figure 5.9**) in the Applications folder on your hard drive. If you are connecting your AirPort Express Base Station to the Internet, you will also need your cable or DSL modem and all the information provided by your Internet service provider.

Figure 5.9

Here's a peek inside what I usually call the "Dreaded Utilities folder" found on your Mac mini. There are programs here that can help you—and some that can really mess up your Mac mini. Unless you know Unix, avoid the Terminal application, especially.

It is generally easier to configure the cable or DSL modem before connecting your base station to it. This way, you can check the broadband connection before adding your base station to the equation.

Follow the directions provided by your cable or DSL company to set up the broadband modem. You will be asked to connect one of your computers to the modem, probably using an Ethernet cable. Your Windows computer may have a built-in Ethernet port that you can use. Or you can use the Ethernet port on the rear panel of your Mac mini.

If you run into problems, call your DSL or cable company for help.

After the broadband connection is working with a single computer, use the AirPort Setup Assistant (**Figure 5.10**) software found in the

Utilities folder on the Mac mini to configure the base station. You will use the same connection settings provided by your cable or DSL company (typically a user name and password) with the base station that you used when connecting a single computer.

Figure 5.10

One of the ways Apple tries to make its customers' lives easier is with the AirPort Setup Utility, used to get your AirPort Extreme or AirPort Express Base Station working properly.

The instructions that come with the AirPort Extreme Base Station are easy to follow and don't bear repeating in this book. You should have no serious problems getting the base station connected and then connecting either Windows computers or Macs to the base station.

Another program, the AirPort Admin Utility (also in Applications > Utilities), makes it easy to change your AirPort base station's internal settings. If you have experience with networks, especially wireless networks, you may find this easier to use than the AirPort Setup Assistant, which is designed for newbie networkers.

Figures 5.11 through **5.17** are a visual tour of the AirPort Admin Utility, showing some of the screens commonly used to administer both the AirPort Extreme and AirPort Express Base Stations.

Figure 5.11

The AirPort Admin Utility gives you access to the settings on all the base stations on your network: in my case, a single AirPort Extreme Base Station and two AirPort Express Base Stations.

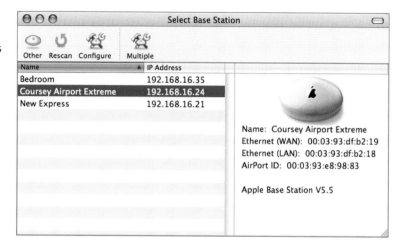

Figure 5.12

This is the AirPort Admin screen used to set up a network on an AirPort Extreme Base Station. In most cases, your settings will look just like these.

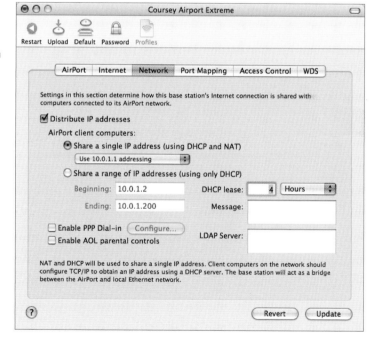

Figure 5.13

This is the AirPort Admin screen used to set up an Internet connection on an AirPort Extreme Base Station. Your Internet service provider will tell you what to enter here. The settings for a "manual" connection can be found by changing the selection from Using DHCP to Manual.

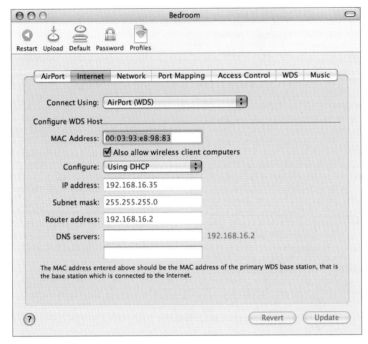

Figure 5.14

Configuring an AirPort Express Base Station is a bit more complex than configuring an AirPort Extreme Base Station. If you use the AirPort Setup Utility, you shouldn't have problems. This screen shows the settings for the AirPort Express in my bedroom.

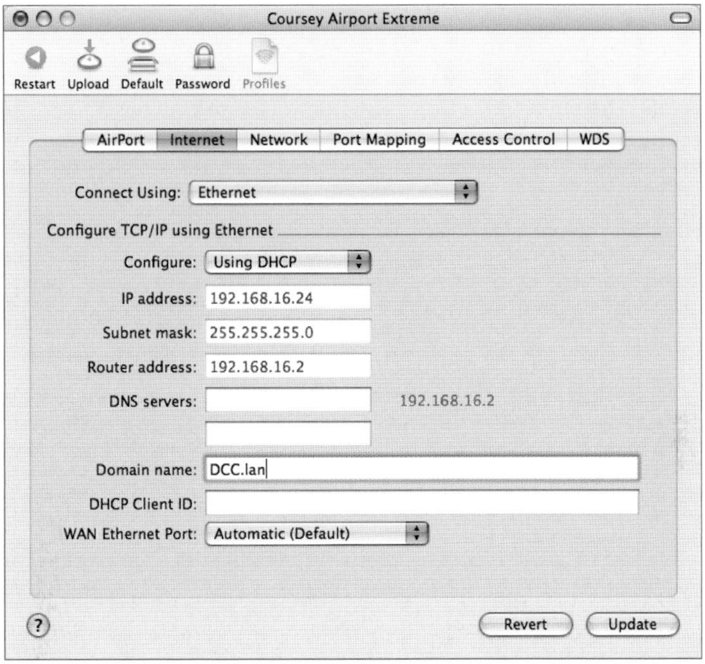

Figure 5.15

This screen is where you set up the AirPort Express Base Station to serve as a relay for other wireless devices, thereby extending the range of your wireless network.

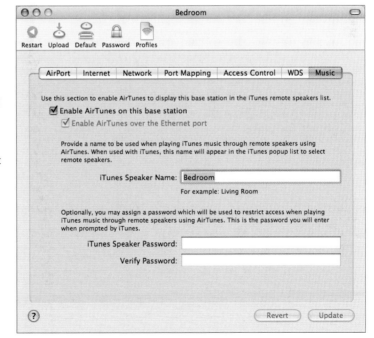

Figure 5.16

One of the AirPort Express Base Station's best features is its ability to play music remotely. iTunes files residing on a Mac mini (or Windows machine, even) can be sent wirelessly to speakers attached to the AirPort Express Base Station.

Figure 5.17

Look inside the dreaded Utility folder and you will find the Network Utility, a collection of Internet services that you may occasionally find useful.

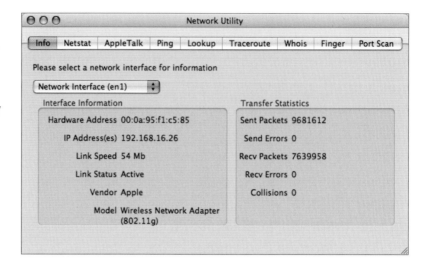

The AirPort Admin Utility also provides access to advanced features. The most useful of these may be the ability to set the channel your network operates on. Normally this isn't necessary, but if you are near other wireless networks or even some cordless telephones, you may wish to change the channel your network uses—this will often help with flaky network connections.

The cordless phones that cause problems are those that operate on 2.4 GHz, which is also the frequency range that 802.11b and 802.11g networks use. Microwave ovens also put out radio frequencies in the 2.4 GHz range. If your wireless network gets fuzzy when you use the microwave, you may want to change the channel and see whether this helps. Check docs.info.apple.com/article.html?artnum=58543 for more information on interference sources.

If you are concerned about people snooping or connecting to your wireless network without your permission, you should turn on something called WEP, or Wireless Encryption Protocol. With WEP, each computer on your network, as well as your AirPort Base Station, must be set to use the same password. Most people don't use WEP, although everyone probably should. To use WEP on an AirPort base station, select the Enable Encryption (Using WEP) check box on the AirPort tab of the AirPort Admin Utility.

I have discovered that the only way to securely and reliably connect Macs to Windows PCs is with 40-bit WEP. I have experimented with the other protocols without success. Read more about WEP in Chapter 7.

If you run into trouble, your cable or DSL provider should be able to help. If not, check the Apple support site or the Genius Bar at your local Apple Store, or send e-mail to coursey@mac.com and I will try to solve your problem.

The Perfect Mac mini and Windows PC Network

The perfect home network, in my estimation, consists of a cable or DSL broadband connection, an AirPort Extreme Base Station, an AirPort card in your Mac mini, and a wireless device for each of your Windows PCs. Add AirPort Express Base Stations as desired.

Ideally, your Windows computer has USB 2.0 ports, which are fast enough to support an 802.11g wireless adapter. If your computer is older and has USB 1.1 ports, you can buy a less-expensive 802.11b USB wireless adapter. It runs at 11 Mbps, about the same speed as the older USB ports.

The AirPort Extreme Base Station uses an Ethernet cable to connect to your DSL or cable modem, which itself connects to a cable or telephone connection. The AirPort Extreme Base Station has an additional Ethernet port that can be used to connect to an Ethernet hub or a single computer. The hub allows multiple computers to be connected using Ethernet cables rather than wirelessly. You can have both wired and wireless computers on the same network.

You will also find a telephone jack on the AirPort Extreme Base Station. This can be connected to a dial-up telephone line and used to connect to America Online. The AOL connection can be accessed across the network, but only by one computer at a time and then only by Macs. This feature also works only in the United States.

The less-perfect Mac mini and Windows PC network

My less-perfect Mac mini and Windows PC network is the same as my "perfect" example except you use some other wireless access point and not an AirPort Extreme Base Station. If you already own a wired or wireless network and connect the Mac mini to it, this is what you have. You will appreciate how easily the Mac mini connects to the network you already own, whether wired or wireless. But please consider upgrading to the AirPort Extreme Base Station.

6

Printing with Your Mac mini

Just as you can continue to use your keyboard, mouse, and display with your Mac mini, you should be able to just plug in your USB printer and start printing. And if you've hooked up an AirPort Wi-Fi network in your home, you can print over that, too. This chapter helps you share a printer between your Mac mini and PC and connect your printer to your AirPort network.

As you read this chapter, you will learn:

- How to connect a printer to your Mac mini.

- How to share a printer between your Mac mini and a PC.

- What your alternatives are if you can't or don't want to share a printer.

- How to connect a USB printer to an Apple AirPort Extreme Base Station or Apple AirPort Express Base Station.

- How to share a printer connected to the AirPort device with both Macintosh and Windows computers.

- How to use Apple's Bonjour/Rendezvous technology for printing.

Connecting a printer to a Mac mini is usually pretty simple—plug it in, select Print in your application, and voilà!—print happens. But you have both a Mac and a Windows PC and want to print from both of them, right? This chapter shows you how.

How to Connect a Printer to Your Mac mini

Connecting a printer to any Macintosh is usually a pleasant surprise: You plug a USB printer into a USB port on the Mac, and the next time you try to print, it just happens.

You will not see the same sort of installation routine Windows goes through when you connect a new piece of hardware to your Mac mini. This sometimes surprises people—including me—the first time it occurs. Yes, just plug in the printer and it works.

This easy connection is possible because Mac OS X arrives with many printer drivers already installed—an excellent example of how Apple tries to make things easy. Why should users have to worry about installing printers? So Mac OS X performs printer installation behind the scenes if the drivers are available.

 tip   Mac OS X comes with drivers for more than 250 printer models already installed, probably including yours. Visit www.apple.com/macosx/ upgrade/printers.html to see the list.

The Print dialog and printer list

When you select the Print command in any Mac OS X application, you will be presented with a Print dialog (**Figure 6.1**). The Print dialog includes a Printer pop-up menu that lists all printers installed on your Macintosh. Choose the one you wish to use. Change any other settings as necessary.

Figure 6.1

This is the Print dialog that was presented to me when I printed a copy of this chapter. SamsungM is a printer that's actually attached to a Windows computer. I could have selected one of the other printers available to the Mac mini. Note the PDF button that is actually a pop-up menu on the bottom of the sheet. You might want to explore all the choices available here. The look of the Print dialog varies slightly from application to application.

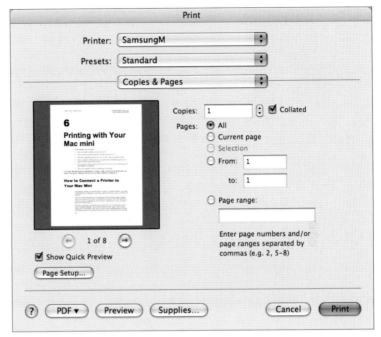

How to Install a USB Printer

Occasionally you may want to use a printer for which Mac OS X doesn't already have drivers installed. You will know the drivers aren't installed if the just-plugged-in printer does not appear in the pop-up window on the Printer dialog.

If the new printer isn't listed, you must install the proper drivers for it to operate. These are typically included on a CD that is included with the printer. Drivers are also available from the printer company's Web site. Only users with an administrator account can install software.

tip Even if Mac OS X automatically installs the new printer, you may still want to go to the printer manufacturer's Web site to see whether updated drivers are available. Or just leave well enough alone since Mac drivers don't change very often.

Usually, installing the driver solves the problem, and the printer will then appear in the pop-up menu. You install a Bonjour/Rendezvous or

Windows-networked printer in the same way. I often print from my Macs to printers connected to my Windows Small Business Server.

note   The Mac OS X 10.4 Tiger operating system makes printing even easier than in previous versions of the OS. If you run into problems, open the Printer Setup Utility (in the Utilities folder in the Applications folder) and follow the instructions in its help file. I've run through several scenarios and found the help, well, extremely, helpful.

About the Printer Setup Utility

If you run into a printer problem, such as being unable to find a printer that is hooked up to your computer, open the Printer Setup Utility, in the Utilities folder on the hard drive of your Mac mini (**Figure 6.2**).

Figure 6.2

The Printer Setup Utility, on the Mac mini's hard drive, is the one-stop shop for solving printing problems. It comes with useful help files, but Mac printing is usually so simple that you may never need to look at them.

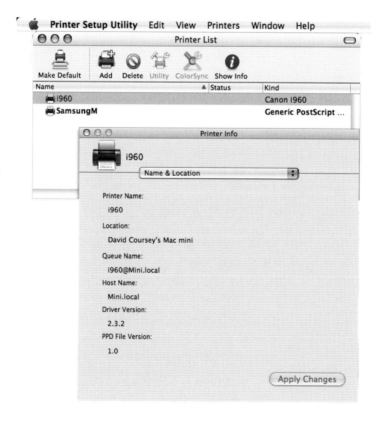

You can also get to these settings from the Print & Fax preferences pane in System Preferences (click the System Preferences icon in your Dock; for information on the Dock, see Chapter 8). If you own more than one Mac and want to share a printer that is attached to one (or more) of them, be sure to turn on Printer Sharing in the Sharing preferences pane.

How to Share a Printer

There are a handful of ways to connect a printer so that it can be shared between your Mac mini and a Windows PC. Here, I will show you eight of them, starting with three that solve the printer-sharing problem by sharing the document to be printed instead of the printer.

1. Mail the file to yourself.

Simply e-mail the document, photograph, or whatever else you want to print from the computer you're using to one that has a printer. E-mail the document to yourself on one machine and open the e-mail on the other. Or mail the document from one e-mail account to another, such as from your .Mac e-mail to your AOL e-mail account. The computer with the printer attached must be able to open the file format you've sent. (See item 3 for a workaround if you can't open the file.) You may not want to e-mail really huge files, but this method works for most files.

2. Save the file to a flash drive.

If you don't want to e-mail the file, you can use a USB flash drive (**Figure 6.3**) to move your files from one machine to another. Flash drives are easy to use and can handle big files, up to the size of the flash drive. These devices, sized to fit on a key chain and available in sizes up to a gigabyte or more, are the floppy disks of the twenty-first century.

You can also burn the file to be printed onto a CD or even copy it onto a compact flash or other memory card, provided you have a reader that works on both computers. A USB card reader can be moved from one computer to another as needed, much like a USB flash drive.

Figure 6.3

This is a Lexar
JumpDrive Expression,
a USB 2.0 flash drive,
that includes three
interchangeable "mood
bands"; pistachio (also
called lime) is shown.
The other colors are
orange and periwinkle.
(Courtesy Lexar)

 tip

An iPod shuffle (**Figure 6.4**) is really just a (very) glorified USB flash
drive and can be used to move files from one computer to another. If
you are thinking about buying a flash drive anyway, getting an iPod
shuffle is a nice upgrade that turns a single-use item into a multitasker.

Figure 6.4

The iPod shuffle can
carry your files as
easily as it carries your
iTunes. (Courtesy Apple
Computer)

3. Use Adobe Acrobat.

If it's the Windows machine that lacks a printer, you can save your document as a PDF (Portable Document Format) file on the Mac mini and print the PDF file using Adobe Reader software on the PC. Mac OS X uses Adobe's PostScript technology internally so it also has the built-in ability to "Save as PDF" from the Print dialog. Creating a PDF file is a handy way to send someone a document when the person may not have the application necessary to open it (**Figure 6.5**).

Figure 6.5

This is the Print dialog where I am about to choose Save as PDF from the PDF pop-up menu. Then I will be asked to save the PDF document, after which the Acrobat document will be created. If you don't know what application a person will use to open your document—and the person won't need to edit your document— use Save as PDF to create an easy-to-e-mail Acrobat file that can be opened by the free Adobe Reader. (You can also purchase Adobe Acrobat for your Windows PC and create PDF files on that computer as well.)

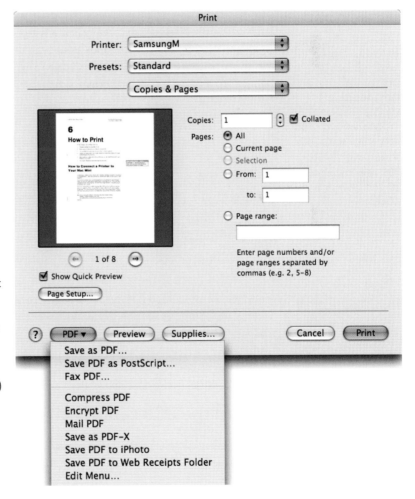

PDF files aren't just useful for printing, of course. Acrobat is an excellent go-between when you create a document in a Mac application for which no PC version exists, and vice versa. Acrobat also provides some assurance that the file won't be changed by the recipient. **Figure 6.6** shows a PDF file open on a Mac mini. It would look the same on a PC running Acrobat Reader.

Figure 6.6

Just so you can see the application, this is an early draft of this chapter that was saved as a PDF file and then opened in Adobe Acrobat 7.0 Professional. There is also a less-expensive Standard version of the program and a free Adobe Reader. Acrobat is a great application if you often share documents with other people.

 The Adobe Acrobat Reader is available free for a variety of operating systems, including the various Windows flavors. Visit www.adobe.com/products/acrobat/readermain.html. In Mac OS X, you don't even need Reader: You can view PDFs with the Preview application in the Applications folder.

4. Swap the USB cable between computers.

My "simple and dopey" way to share a printer uses the Armstrong Method: Use your arm (and hand) to unplug the USB printer cable from one computer and insert it into another.

Many recent PCs have USB ports on the front panel, which makes the connection easy at that end. If your Mac mini has a USB hub attached, the printer USB cable can be inserted there. This beats having to reach behind the Mac mini and plug into that USB port every time you want to print.

5. Use a printer with both parallel and USB connections.

Another easy way to share a printer between a PC and a Mac mini is to use a printer with both parallel and USB connections. You can connect a USB cable to the Mac and a parallel cable to the PC. This usually works well.

 Not all printers have both USB and parallel ports, so this option may not be available to you. Parallel printer ports are slowly disappearing as USB becomes ever more popular.

6. Use a KVM switch with a built-in USB hub.

If you have a KVM switch that includes USB switching, you can connect the USB printer cable to the switch, and then whichever computer is active on your screen will also be connected to the printer.

The Belkin Omniview SOHO Series two-port KVM switch with audio discussed in Chapter 4 includes this feature. It will switch two USB ports between two computers; use one for the printer and the second for something else.

KVM switches are discussed in detail in Chapter 4.

7. Use a USB switch.

You can purchase a switch that allows a single USB device to be switched between several computers. I am not sure why you would use a USB switch, but it provides another way to share a printer.

8. Use an AirPort Extreme or AirPort Express wireless network.

The AirPort Extreme and AirPort Express wireless network base stations each include a USB printer port. The printer attached to the base station can be used by both Macs and PCs connected to the wireless network. It will appear on your Macs as a Bonjour printer. You may need to use the Printer Setup Utility, found on your hard drive, to add the printer to your Mac mini.

On a Windows machine, you must install the Bonjour technology (previously called Rendezvous) to connect to the shared printer. You'll find more about the AirPort Extreme and AirPort Express Base Stations in Chapter 5. There you will also find information about connecting your Mac mini to a new or existing wireless network.

tip Not all printers are compatible with the USB port used by AirPort Extreme and AirPort Express. Apple seems to have stopped keeping an official compatibility list. This is good news since it means that Apple doesn't consider compatibility to be an issue any more. You can find a list of AirPort-compatible USB printers at www.efelix.co.uk/tech/ 1013.html. Or visit www.peachpit.com/coursey for a page that includes all the links in this book, organized by chapter.

How to Connect Your Mac mini to a Bonjour Printer

To connect your Mac mini to a Bonjour (formerly Rendezvous) printer, follow these steps:

1. If the printer drivers are not already installed on your Mac mini, install them, either from the CD that came with your printer or from the manufacturer's Web site. It is generally a good idea to check the manufacturer's Web site for new drivers even if Mac OS X has the driver preinstalled.

2. Open the Print dialog. In the pop-up Printer menu, look for the shared printer (**Figure 6.7**).

Figure 6.7

This is how you select a Bonjour or other shared printer from the print dialog.

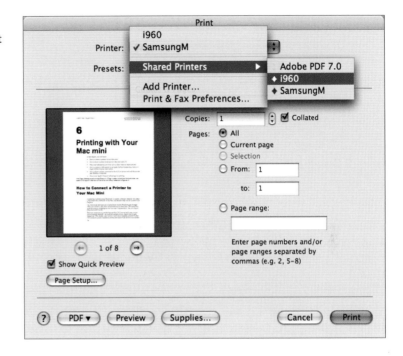

How to Install Bonjour/Rendezvous for Windows

Apple has a version of Bonjour/Rendezvous for Windows XP and Windows 2000 that it makes available at its developer Web site. As I write, Apple refers to the version now available as "Rendezvous for Windows Technology Preview 4." This is Apple's way of saying that the software isn't fully tested, but it worked just fine for me.

Bonjour/Rendezvous for Windows can be downloaded from developer.apple.com/macosx/rendezvous/. Though it's described as a "preview" (that is, beta) version, it has worked fine for me.

You install the Bonjour/Rendezvous software just as you would any other Windows application. The Technology Preview installs a Printer Setup wizard on your Windows machine. When asked whether you want a shortcut placed on your desktop, respond Yes.

What Is Bonjour?

In Mac OS X Tiger, Apple changed the name of a technology called Rendezvous to Bonjour. Both are pretty silly names for some pretty serious technology. There is no difference between Bonjour and Rendezvous. Be aware that it may be a while before the Windows version gets a name change.

Apple describes Bonjour this way: "Bonjour lets you create an instant network of computers and smart devices just by getting them connected to each other." After that, the devices start broadcasting and discovering the services each is offering to the others.

Bonjour is based on standard Internet technologies, and Apple has offered it to be adopted as a standard. I hope this happens and encourage Microsoft to adopt Bonjour (or whatever the "standard" version is finally called) as a Windows component.

Apple uses Bonjour for tasks as diverse as instant messaging and sharing printers and files. Thanks to Bonjour, the iChat AV instant messaging program can tell you what other users are currently on your local network and the types of chat—text, audio, or video—their computers support. iTunes and iPhoto use Bonjour to support music and photo sharing on local networks.

Note that I am talking about Macs and local networks. At the time of this writing, only a Bonjour Printer Setup wizard is available for Microsoft Windows. The wizard installs the Bonjour technology on your Windows machine and makes it easy to connect to a printer that itself is connected to the USB port on an Apple AirPort base station or to AirPort Express.

If you own several Macs, Bonjour is important technology. Apple has begun extending it to the Windows world, where it could play an important role in powering the home media environment of the future. Maybe Microsoft will come on board some day and speed the process. Bonjour is good stuff!

The software will ask you to reboot your Windows machine once the installation is complete. You might as well do so then because you won't see the shortcut to the wizard until you've restarted your PC.

 If anyone with sway over Bill Gates should read this, ask him to build Bonjour/Rendezvous support into Microsoft operating systems. It has the potential to make Windows almost as easy to use as Mac OS X, at least in some ways.

After installing the wizard, I recommend installing the proper Windows drivers for the printer that's connected to the AirPort Extreme Base Station or to AirPort Express. If this is the same printer you've been using previously with Windows, the machine won't need new drivers.

You will, however, need to download Mac OS X drivers from the printer manufacturer's Web site. Be warned that not all printers have Mac OS X drivers available, though if you are using a major-brand printer, you are probably covered.

How to Install a Bonjour/ Rendezvous Printer on Your Windows PC

To install a Bonjour/Rendezvous printer on your PC, start the wizard, and it will go looking for your printer and, upon finding it, allow you to select the printer and then install it. The process really should be that simple. Follow the on-screen directions.

If things go reasonably well, you will have all this installation work done—from downloading the Windows software to getting the printer working with *both* the Mac mini and your Windows PC—in about 10 minutes.

7

Protecting
Your Mac mini

Although the Mac OS is much more secure than Windows, that doesn't mean you can stop paying attention. You should take a couple of sensible steps to protect your Mac and your wireless network, if you have one, from data loss and prying eyes.

As you read this chapter, you will learn:

- The importance of backing up your important files, and how to do it.

- How to stop viruses, hackers, and other threats.

- How to protect your Mac mini.

- How to protect your network, whether wired or wireless.

- Why Macs are more secure than Windows machines.

My friend Charlie Wolf—the securities analyst who estimated that 225,000 Mac minis were sold in the model's first three months on the market—noticed something interesting during his research. When he asked people why they were buying a Mac mini, he heard one answer over and over: security.

Word has gotten out that Mac OS X is tremendously more secure than Windows, and Windows users appear to have gotten the message.

So if you're here because you are sick and tired of being drawn into Microsoft's security battles, welcome! While no computer is completely secure, Mac OS X is a much more secure operating system than anything Microsoft publishes. It may not always be that way, but for now that's a big win for Mac users.

While researching this book, I spoke with the Mac product manager of an antivirus and security software company whose name most PC users would recognize. He told me that his company—which usually knows all things about all threats—*is aware of no viruses or malware that specifically target Mac OS X.*

 This chapter talks only about threats to the Mac mini and other Macintosh computers. It does not offer any advice about keeping your Windows computers safe.

Not long ago, I noticed that I'd been running an iMac for two years with the virus protection turned off. Okay, I didn't run the iMac all the time, but often enough. Had the computer been a PC instead of a Mac, I am sure I'd have been in deep trouble.

When I noticed my error, I immediately installed new antivirus software and ran a full scan of the hard drive. No viruses were found.

Does that mean I've decided to run my Macs without antivirus software? Not on your life. There's a difference between getting away with something and pressing your luck. Running any computer without virus protection is definitely a case of the latter.

I don't believe the "no viruses/no malware" situation can last forever. On the other hand, I am not going to worry about my Mac mini as much as I do about my Windows machines.

In this chapter, I outline my personal security strategy and offer suggestions for what you should do to protect your Mac mini as well as the wireless network I hope you've installed. Of the two, I consider the network to be much more at risk.

Simple Things to Do Right Now

Here is a list of some very simple things you can do right, this very moment, to make your Mac mini better protected from the various forces of evil arrayed against it. The first two suggestions are *really* important.

1. Turn off automatic login.

I know it's convenient not to have to enter a password when you start your computer. But unless you trust everyone who might have access to your Mac mini, you should require a password to start the machine.

Protect yourself: Go to the Mac OS X Accounts System Preferences pane and deselect the "Automatically log in as" option (**Figure 7.1**).

Figure 7.1

What's wrong here? If you expect any measure of security, you must disable automatic login. So you will see it, I've allowed it here, but I immediately unchecked it as soon as I grabbed the screen image for this book. Remember: Keep this check box clear. You can disable automatic login for all users in item 3, below.

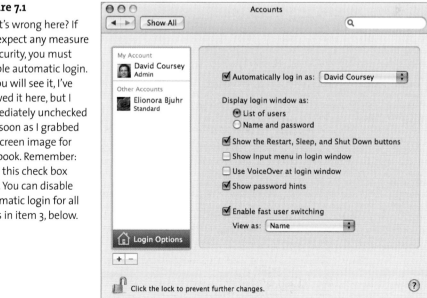

2. Create individual user accounts.

Give everyone who uses your Mac mini a separate account, and no one will be messing around while logged in as you. Messing around includes looking at your files and installing software.

To add an account, go to the Mac OS X Accounts pane and click the + sign. Note that you can limit what can be done from each account, including what applications the person using the account can run and whether the account user can change any settings. New in Mac OS X 10.4 Tiger are parental control settings (**Figure 7.2**).

Figure 7.2

Once you create a user, you can select the parental controls you want to invoke. These can limit who the user exchanges e-mail with and what Web sites the user can visit and can even screen some profanity from the Dictionary application.

3. Require a password when your Mac mini wakes up from sleep or a screen saver.

When you walk away from your machine, it may hide your work by launching a screen saver or going to sleep, but it will wake right up if someone touches your keyboard. Once awake, your Mac is wide open to exploration by, well, anybody who can get to it.

Protect yourself: Go to the Security System Preferences pane and select "Require password to wake this computer from sleep or screen saver." Now when your machine wakes up, you will be asked for your password to resume work.

Also disable automatic login, which will prevent any user from logging in automatically. (See Item 1.)

Hint: You can set how long the machine must sit idle before the screen saver or sleep mode kicks in. You want it to be short enough that your machine doesn't spend large amounts of time unprotected when you're away but long enough that you don't have to keep reentering your password because the screen saver starts every time you get a phone call (**Figure 7.3**).

Figure 7.3

The Security System Preferences pane allows you to change a number of settings affecting all users of your Mac mini. It's important to require a password to wake up the computer and to keep your FileVault master password secure (yet memorable). This is also where you can prevent any user from automatically logging in.

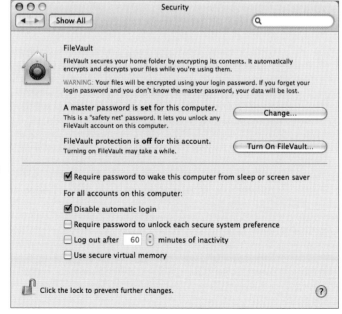

4. Use FileVault.

FileVault is a feature built in to Mac OS X that can encrypt your home folder. This encryption completely protects your files even if someone steals your computer. To use FileVault, visit the Security System Preferences pane. Note that if you are the administrator of your Mac mini, you will be asked to create a master password that can open any user's FileVault-protected home folder. This master password is used when the user forgets his or her own password or when the administrator wants to see what a user has been doing. Thus, FileVault offers complete protection only if you are the administrator. Also, FileVault automatically opens the encrypted home folder when the user logs in, so anybody who has the user's password has access to the user's files.

Remember to keep the master password safe (**Figure 7.4**).

Figure 7.4
Read and heed the warning about what happens if you lose your master FileVault password.

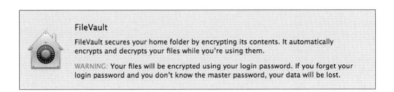

5. Use a more secure password.

I don't know any "normal" people who use proper passwords—that is passwords that essentially look like random characters and are at least 10 characters long. The problem with these passwords is that they are almost impossible to remember so users write them down, sometimes on Post-it notes stuck to the computer itself.

My recommendation is to use multiple passwords. Have one to use in circumstances where you don't mind giving the password to friends or co-workers. At the other extreme, have a password you wouldn't tell your priest.

For your most secure password, avoid dictionary words, names, and any information that might be discoverable about you. This includes your mother's maiden name, old street addresses, and telephone numbers. Never use your social security number for anything. Use a collection of letters, numbers, and characters. Perhaps this will be something you can refer to later so you can remember where the password came from even if you can't remember the password itself. An example might be the first letter from every line in a favorite poem with some numbers or punctuation thrown in.

6. Completely erase your files.

When you empty the Trash on your Mac mini, you make filenames disappear, but the data remains on your hard drive. From the Finder menu, select Secure Empty Trash (**Figure 7.5**), and your Mac mini will both empty the Trash and write over the files so they are unreadable with file recovery software.

Figure 7.5
Here's how you make sure your trash is really gone. Selecting Secure Empty Trash from the Finder menu both dumps the trash and overwrites the files you've thrown away.

7. And for the really paranoid...

I won't talk about this in detail, but you can set a password that must be entered before your Mac mini will boot up (and way before you normally enter your password). To find out how to set an *open firmware* password, visit the Apple Web site and do a search. If you forget this password, you are *really* hosed, okay?

Do as I Do? (But at Your Own Risk!)

The Peachpit Press attorneys have persuaded me to advise you of the following: If you follow my advice and something bad happens, it's not Peachpit's fault or my fault. You're a grown-up and need to make your own decisions.

Still, I can't in good conscience tell you to spend $150 on software intended to protect you from questionable threats. Heck, I get this software *for free*, and all you will find running on my Macs are antivirus software and the built-in Mac OS X firewall. I have never had a virus problem on a Mac.

I think the companies that sell security software overdramatize the risk that Macs face. They do this to make a buck and justify it by saying that they are just offering a "prudent" level of protection to their customers.

If you visit the Intego Web site—Intego is an antivirus and firewall company—and don't feel frightened, you are stronger than I am. But remember that Intego's goal is to make your wallet $150 lighter. A visit to www.intego.com is not for the faint-hearted.

I lose much more sleep over the security of my Windows network—which is doubly protected in some areas—than I would over a *completely unprotected* Mac. Not that you shouldn't buy some protection—you definitely should; this is just a personal assessment of the comparative threat facing Microsoft Windows versus Mac OS X.

About Backing Up

In this section, I talk about all sorts of mostly potential threats to a Mac mini. But I just mentioned the most important threat—and did so almost in passing. So here goes:

More data is lost to operator error and hard drive failure than all other causes combined.

You should protect yourself by making at least occasional backups of all your computers—especially important for users who have invested many hours and a lot of money building music and family photography collections they'd hate to see disappear.

The way to protect your files is to copy the data to another hard drive or onto DVDs. A .Mac membership buys you a program called Backup as well as remote storage on .Mac's iDisk. You should use both.

The Backup software makes it easy to safeguard your important data, though not your applications. The iDisk gives you a place to store your most important files on the Internet, where they are safe from such dangers as the loss of your computer or your house burning down. **Figures 7.6**, **7.7**, and **7.8** illustrate the .Mac backup features.

Figure 7.6

The Backup utility provided with a .Mac membership allows you to save copies of your data to a variety of targets, including external hard drives, other Macs, your .Mac iDisk, and a CD or DVD disc, as shown here.

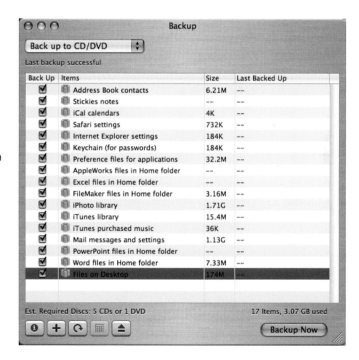

Back Up	Items	Size	Last Backed Up
☑	Address Book contacts	6.21M	--
☑	Stickies notes	--	--
☑	iCal calendars	4K	--
☑	Safari settings	732K	--
☑	Internet Explorer settings	184K	--
☑	Keychain (for passwords)	184K	--
☑	Preference files for applications	32.2M	--
☑	AppleWorks files in Home folder	--	--
☑	Excel files in Home folder	--	--
☑	FileMaker files in Home folder	3.16M	--
☑	iPhoto library	1.71G	--
☑	iTunes library	15.4M	--
☑	iTunes purchased music	36K	--
☑	Mail messages and settings	1.13G	--
☑	PowerPoint files in Home folder	--	--
☑	Word files in Home folder	7.33M	--
☑	Files on Desktop	174M	--

Back up to CD/DVD

Last backup successful

Est. Required Discs: 5 CDs or 1 DVD   17 Items, 3.07 GB used

Backup Now

Figure 7.7

When you use Backup with your iDisk, you'll want to make the items list shorter to better match the limited capacity of the iDisk, shown at the top right. An iDisk backup is perfect for frequently changed items, such as documents, and can be set to run automatically, as shown at the bottom left.

Figure 7.8

.Mac Sync is a feature added with Mac OS X 10.4 Tiger that allows multiple Macs to remain synchronized via the .Mac service. Because this allows your data to be stored on .Mac, it's an effective backup approach, even if you don't have other Macs to share data with.

Here's what I do:

I run regular backups of my files, using Backup to store them on an external FireWire hard drive. Such drives are fairly inexpensive and can be used for many storage tasks.

When I download software, I store a copy on the external drive.

My most important documents end up in three places: on iDisk (using Backup), on the external drive (Backup again), and on my iPod shuffle or another USB drive. Sometimes I do this manually, and sometimes I use a synchronization program.

The only way to truly protect your important files is to make a backup and take the backup someplace else. Having files on an external hard drive is great protection against primary drive failure but won't help if your house burns and both drives go with it.

tip **If you are buying an external hard drive, make sure you get one that will connect to both your Mac mini and your Windows computers. Since the Mac mini has both USB 2.0 and FireWire ports, and many PCs have only USB, a USB drive is the safest choice. However, older PCs will have USB 1.1 ports that are too slow to use with an external drive.**

Rarely, I will make a DVD backup (again using Backup) that goes into a fire-resistant safe. I could also ask a neighbor to keep these or put them in a safe-deposit box at the bank.

There are programs that allow you to copy music from your iPod back onto a Macintosh, but I—thankfully—have never needed one, so I can't make a recommendation as to which is best.

Backup is a good reason to get a .Mac subscription. However, if you have a more complex situation—for instance, if you want to back up both Macs and PCs—or if you simply don't like Backup, then consider a program called Retrospect, discussed in Chapter 10. It is powerful, yet easy to use. Single-user copies are often provided free with new hard drives. Visit www.retrospect.com for more information.

Security Bundles

Both Intego and Symantec offer a collection of security products that include antivirus, firewall, and various other security applications in a single package. One is Intego's super-duper, diamond-studded Platinum package, which comes with an equally inflated $150 price tag.

Symantec offers Norton Internet Security 3.0 for Macintosh, which is priced at $100 and represents the better value. Besides the firewall and antivirus software, the Norton package includes parental control software and an application that protects information you've flagged as "sensitive" from going out over the Internet without explicit permission.

Intego lives at www.intego.com. You will find Symantec at www.symantec.com.

Specific Threats Defeated

This section catalogs various threats and describes how to deal with them.

Viruses, Trojans, and other malware

To protect my Macs against what I will collectively call "viruses," I use two products—not all on the same machine, but I have been doing a long-term comparison of them on the different Macs that I use each day. The problem is that with few, if any, real Mac OS X threats, it's hard to say one works better than the other.

There are two antivirus programs for Mac that I recommend. Either of them will do a fine job of protecting your Mac mini.

(A third program I used to recommend—McAfee Virex—does not at this time run on Mac OS X 10.4. It works great on Mac OS X 10.3 and earlier versions, though. Until Tiger, it was part of the annual .Mac package, and if you are running it on Mac OS X 10.3, you ca[n] use Virex and receive updates to virus definitions through May 2006.)

They are:

Intego VirusBarrier X (Figure 7.9). This is a nice package with an above-average user interface. *Macworld* magazine says that of the two programs I recommend, it is the faster at scanning a hard drive. Check it out at www.intego.com.

Figure 7.9
Intego VirusBarrier X.

Symantec Norton AntiVirus (Figure 7.10). This is the program I use on both Macs and Windows machines and have used forever. The company updates its software every Thursday, and the software does a good job of removing PC viruses that sometimes lurk in the Mac mini's Mail folders. This benefit is valuable because it protects you from viruses that land on your Mac and then somehow wind up on your PC (or get sent to someone else).

Figure 7.10

It's hard to show all the features of Norton AntiVirus in a single screen shot, but this image gives you some idea of the available options.

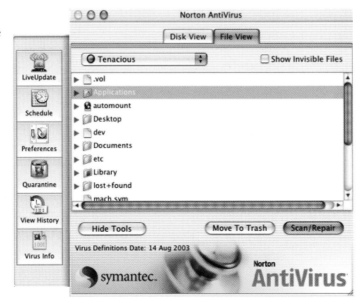

Hackers

There is a small possibility that someone out on the Internet will break into your Mac mini and steal personal information or do damage. Viruses and other malware can also do this.

To protect yourself against this threat, you need a firewall. Fortunately, you already have one, included as part of Mac OS X on your Mac mini. Your job is to make sure it's turned on and the proper settings have been chosen.

A firewall prevents your Mac from being attacked from the Internet while still allowing your mail, instant messenger, browser, and other applications to function properly.

In early 2005, *Macworld* magazine did a comparative review of several Mac firewalls, finding them all inadequate to protect the user's computer against an attack by a well-motivated (that is, profit minded) adversary.

So bearing in mind that no firewall offers complete protection, there remain three that I recommend. They range in price from free to $70. They are:

Apple's built-in Mac OS X firewall. The built-in firewall lacks bells, whistles, and some level of functionality. But it works just fine, and the price is right. You'll find it in System Preferences' Sharing pane. For more on the firewall, see www.apple.com (**Figure 7.11**).

Intego NetBarrier. Of the three firewalls mentioned here, NetBarrier provides the highest level of protection. It costs $70 if purchased alone. Check it out at www.intego.com.

Symantec Norton Personal Firewall. Like NetBarrier, this program offers greater protection than the Mac's built-in firewall and gives you insight into what it's doing at any given moment. If you are going to spend $70 for the Norton antivirus software away, you can get this firewall and a privacy/parental control program for $30 more. Not a bad investment if you have the money to spend.

The Norton firewall also sells for $70. Get the idea they are telling you something with this pricing? Like, "buy the bundle"?

Figure 7.11

The built-in Mac OS X firewall is accessed from the Sharing System Preferences pane. Note the items that are checked, which are located at the bottom of the scrolling menu. These must be selected for the service to function and are easily overlooked.

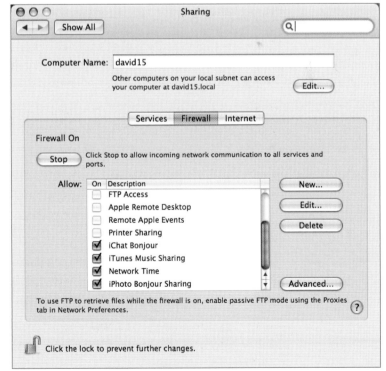

How to Use Your Mac mini's Built-in Firewall

The purpose of a firewall is to block unwanted and potentially harmful network communications with your computer. You can use the built-in firewall to protect the services available for Mac OS X. These include Personal File Sharing, Windows Sharing, Personal Web Sharing, Remote Login, FTP Access, Apple Remote Desktop, Remote Apple Events, and Printer Sharing.

Here's what each does:

Personal File Sharing: Allows you to share files with other Macintoshes on your network.

Windows Sharing: Allows you to share files with other Windows computers on your network.

Personal Web Sharing: Allows others on a network to access pages you have created that live on your Mac mini. Running under the hood of your Mac mini is an Apache Web server. If you want others on your network to have access to Web pages you have created, you must select this option. The address of your Web site appears in the window when you select this option. To learn more, visit Apple's Mac OS X support site.

Remote Login: Allows you to log into your Mac mini from across the network. You aren't likely to use this.

FTP Access: Allows file transfers using the FTP protocol. You aren't likely to use this.

Apple Remote Desktop: Allows remote access to your computer from another Mac running the Apple Remote Desktop application.

Remote Apple Events: Allows program-to-program communication that I've never needed.

Printer Sharing: Allows a printer attached to your Mac mini to be shared with other computers on your network.

Xgird: Allows your Mac to work with other Macs on a network to process a task. You really aren't likely to use this.

If the firewall is turned on, only the selected services will be allowed, and other communication with your Mac mini will be denied.

How to Use Your Mac mini's Built-in Firewall *(continued)*

To enable the built-in firewall:

1. Open System Preferences and click Sharing.

2. On the Services pane, you will see the list of services. Click those you want to enable. If the service is not turned on, it will not be accessible from other computers either on your local network or the Internet.

3. Click Firewall to turn on the firewall. Select the same services as those you selected in the Services pane.

Important: Note that iChat Bonjour and iTunes Music Sharing appear at the bottom on the list. Select one or both of these if you intend to use them. And if you don't select them now, remember to revisit these settings if you later decide to use these features. If you try to share your iTunes music library across your network and it doesn't work, this is the first place to check.

The Firewall pane also allows you to add settings for other services and applications, which I have never needed to do on a Macintosh.

The Internet pane allows you to share an Internet connection with other computers on your network. I don't recommend using this method to share your connection.

Adware and spyware

As mentioned earlier, at this writing there is no known adware or spyware threat lurking on the Internet waiting for some Mac mini to happen by, so you really don't—right now, anyway—need an adware/spyware detection program for your Mac mini.

At present, the best protection against infectious spyware and adware is a good firewall. The Mac's Safari browser has a setting to stop pop-ups from appearing while you're surfing the Internet. Firefox, another popular Mac browser, also protects you against pop-ups.

note **Microsoft is no longer building Internet Explorer for Macintosh.**

Snoopers and identity thieves

If you have already followed the suggestions earlier in this chapter, you are well ahead of most people in protecting personal information stored on your Mac mini.

There is, however, one more thing you might want to do and that's install some sort of privacy management software. Norton Privacy Control, which comes with the Norton Internet Security 3.0 package, protects personal information from being sent without your knowledge and permission. This keeps your credit card numbers, social security number, and other most-personal information out of the hands of bad guys. The software watches your Internet connection, and if it sees any of this information going out, it stops the data until you give permission for it to be sent. The software also blocks JavaScript pop-ups.

You might also want to look at two programs that protect your privacy by cleaning various files off your Mac mini that could tell a snooper what you've been up to. These programs don't do things that you couldn't do without their help. There is, however, something to be said for automation (especially if you tend to forget what to delete and where to find it). They are:

Internet Cleanup, $29.99 (Allume Systems, www.allume.com).

MacWasher X, $29.95 (Webroot Software, www.webroot.com).

Attacks by mail

There are many ways to get some protection from spam, usually by using a filter. This can be installed on the mail server you use or on your own machine. If you have a free e-mail account or get one from .Mac or your Internet service provider, you get some level of spam protection. The Mail program that is included with your Mac mini provides some protection as well.

Phishing is something we all need to work together to fight—which means telling people about the threat. By this, I mean telling older people, new users, kids, and anyone else who might be tempted by a legit-looking e-mail that asks for banking or other financial information not to provide it.

I receive dozens of these messages a day, usually "from" banks, other institutions, and online services where I don't even have an account. So do lots of my friends, and the bad guys keep sending more, so they must be working with someone. Don't respond, and don't let someone you know respond either!

Why Is a Mac More Secure than a PC?

One reason that Macs are more secure than other systems is that Apple has designed Mac OS X to be more secure than other operating systems you might immediately think of. For example, having to enter your administrator password to install software may seem like a bother sometimes, but it reduces the potential for dangerous software to install itself while you aren't paying attention.

In the Windows world, some people are advocating a switch to "least privilege" computing. That's where users have only the rights necessary to run the programs they are using. Users can't do things like install software and change settings, which is how the bad guys do their damage.

This seems like a no-brainer, except that many Windows programs require administrator rights just to run. This allows viruses and other malware to do all sorts of damage that would be impossible if only the more limited "user" rights were being enforced. I know that seems dumb now, but when Windows programmers first started writing their programs to require administrator rights, there weren't any threats to take advantage of this approach.

Partially because it's based on Unix and partially because of choices by Apple engineers, Mac OS X works in a "least privilege" manner without all the logging in and logging out. All it asks is that you occasionally enter your administrator password.

Mac OS X 10.4 Tiger also warns users when they download a program file, allowing them to head off many potential threats from downloaded software.

A second reason Mac OS X is more secure than Microsoft Windows is because the hobby hackers don't hate Apple and they do hate Microsoft. Writing a Mac virus isn't as likely to make the news or earn the respect of hacker buddies as doing something to bring the mighty Microsoft Windows to its knees.

The third and final reason is that Apple isn't a very big target. Let's say you are a criminal hacker and want to do something that commits as large a crime as possible—perhaps by spreading spyware. Which do you target: Windows or Mac OS X? The choice is obvious, and it's the one that criminals make.

However, if Apple gains some traction in the marketplace with the Mac mini and sales of Macs to iPod users, then the opportunities for foul play will increase, and Mac users will be faced with greater challenges than they must deal with today. This potential scenario is why I recommend that Mac users invest in commercial antivirus software and consider the purchase of a firewall if they are concerned that Apple's built-in firewall does not provide enough protection.

Wireless Security Issues

In Chapter 5, I extol the virtues of having a wireless network in your home or small business but only briefly touch on security. Here is a more complete discussion of the subject.

Are AirPort wireless networks secure?

A wireless network is not as secure as a network connected exclusively by wires.

An all-Macintosh network can be made more secure than a network with both Macs and Windows machines, because such a network at present requires compatible security settings, and the Mac offers a wider set of options than Windows.

If your network includes both Macs and PCs and you use the 40-bit WEP encryption provided by the AirPort Extreme Base Station, you are protecting yourself to a very significant degree while maintaining Windows compatibility. You can also hide the name of the network from outsiders and even limit network access to only your own hardware. The AirPort base station also allows you to reduce the transmitter power, thus reducing range and the potential for eavesdropping or unauthorized access.

tip

I am always surprised by how many wide-open networks are out there. These are convenient if you need to check your e-mail and happen to luck into one, but they are potentially bad news for their owners.

My own network is password and 40-bit WEP protected, and while it would be nice to have stronger protection, I am not terribly concerned.

Will other people be able to use my wireless Internet connection?

Other people won't be able to use your wireless connection, but only if you choose a good network password.

For an extra level of security, select "Create a closed network" on the AirPort tab of the AirPort Admin Utility (**Figure 7.12**) to hide the name of the network. A user then must also know the exact name of the AirPort network to join it.

You can also prevent authorized access by telling your AirPort base station to connect only to devices with specific 12-digit AirPort IDs. You will find these numbers on the labels of your AirPort cards; enter the numbers in your AirPort Admin Utility (**Figure 7.13**). You will also find a 12-digit ID on each of your Windows wireless adapters.

Figure 7.12

Selecting the "Create a closed network" option in the AirPort Admin Utility increases security by requiring users to know the name of your network (it's *coursey* in this example) in order to connect.

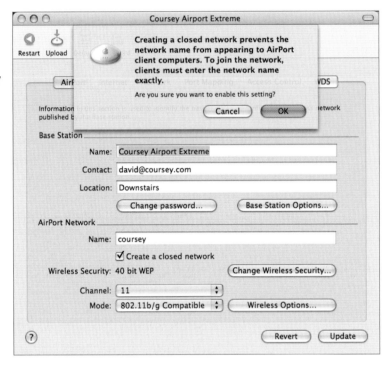

Figure 7.13

You can lock down your network by allowing only certain wireless cards to connect to your AirPort Extreme Base Station. This takes a little effort and makes it difficult for guests to use your wireless network, but it works.

Alternatively, you can do nothing and share your bandwidth with the neighbors. You can do this by either not giving your network a password (a really bad idea) or sharing the password you've created. Do this only if you really trust the people you give the password to and then be ready to change the password on the base station (and all your computers) if the need arises.

As mentioned in Chapter 5, you may run into legal problems if you share your connection. Your agreement with your ISP may include a clause intended to prevent this sort of sharing. In my mind, such sharing, done over the long term, is unethical. It costs a lot of money to install and support a broadband network, and the carriers are entitled to a fair return.

Is my DSL or cable-modem connection secure?

The security of your DSL or cable-modem connection is related to the question of whether you should use a firewall (the answer is yes).

In the Finder, open the Go menu and select Connect to Server. You can then look around the network for anything you don't recognize as your own. Some cable-modem networks are notoriously open, allowing everyone in a neighborhood to see each other's computers. This is why you should use a firewall and strong passwords.

In general, if you don't need file sharing (or any of the other features on the Sharing System Preferences pane), turn it off for greater protection.

8

A Visual Tour of
Mac OS X Tiger

Let's look around Mac OS X 10.4. If you've never used a Mac before, this chapter should get you started. And if you've used previous versions of Mac OS X, it will help you get up to speed with some of the features of the latest version.

As you read this chapter, you will learn:

- Some of the most important features of Mac OS X 10.4 Tiger.

- That your Windows knowledge can quickly translate to your Mac mini.

- About Spotlight and Dashboard, two powerful new Mac OS X features.

Congratulations! If you can operate a Windows PC, you've already done all the hard work involved in learning Mac OS X. Your next step is to sit down at your Mac mini and start exploring.

But first, I hope you'll consider this chapter a travel guide and let me show you the sights of Mac OS X 10.4 Tiger. I've tried to keep the tour short, so there are many things I won't show you. But you will get a taste of your new operating system.

 Tiger was the code name for Mac OS X 10.4, but Apple uses it widely in the product promotion and branding, and it has become the operating system's post-release nickname as well. In case you're interested, Tiger is the fifth in Apple's series of big-cat code names for its operating system releases. It was preceded by Cheetah, Puma, Jaguar, and Panther.

Introducing the Tiger Desktop

Our first stop is the Mac OS X Tiger Desktop (**Figure 8.1**). The figure shows the Mac mini that I used to write most of this book. Your Mac mini screen may look a little different.

Figure 8.1 The Mac OS X Tiger Desktop, generally considered to be a gorgeous user interface.

The items shown on the Mac mini screens in this chapter may be different than those on yours, depending on how you've configured your machine.

The main elements of the Mac desktop include the Dock, which stretches across the bottom of the screen, and the menu bar, which spans the top. You also see the hard drive, which I have renamed so I can easily remember what it is.

The following sections describe the main elements of Mac OS X Tiger.

Dock

The launch bar, or Dock, spread across the bottom of the screen is the first thing most people notice when introduced to Mac OS X. The Dock (**Figure 8.2**) is roughly equivalent to the Start menu in Microsoft Windows. It shows all the applications you are currently running (with triangles under their icons) as well as those whose icons you have dropped onto the Dock for easy access. A single click on the icon starts the application; its icon will bounce as the program starts.

The size and position of the Dock can be changed, as you'll soon see.

Everyone's Dock is a bit different, but, from left to right, here's what is on mine: Finder, Dashboard, iChat AV, Safari browser, Mail, Sherlock, Address Book, iTunes, iCal, iPhoto, Microsoft Word, Excel, PowerPoint, and Trash. Both the Finder and Dashboard have triangles under them, showing that they are running. You will find many of these same icons on your Mac mini when you start it for the first time.

All of the applications except two—the Finder and Dashboard—are discussed in Chapter 9. The Finder and Dashboard are both explained later in this chapter, as is the top menu bar.

Figure 8.2 The Dock is the first thing most people notice when introduced to Mac OS X. It gives users easy access to their most-used applications and also is kind of cute.

Apple Menu

Clicking the Apple icon in the top-left corner opens the Apple menu (**Figure 8.3**). The figure shows the choices available and takes us a bit deeper into the Dock item, showing some of the options (you can display additional Dock items by choosing Dock Preferences).

The Apple menu offers these choices:

- **About This Mac.** Selecting this option opens the About This Mac dialog. If you click the More Info button in this dialog, you open the System Profiler application, which provides technical information about your Mac.

Figure 8.3 The Apple menu is an important part of Mac OS X functionality. It is always in the upper-left corner of the screen.

- **Software Update.** This option is very important as it leads you to updates for your operating system and Apple-branded software. Software Update can, and should, be set to run automatically. You can do this from the Software Update System Preferences pane.

- **Mac OS X Software.** This option takes you to the Apple Web site and a listing of available Mac OS X software.

- **System Preferences.** Choosing this option is equivalent to choosing the Control Panel on a Windows machine. I will show the preferences to you in a moment.

- **Dock.** The submenu (Figure 8.3) gives you access to Dock settings, as discussed previously.

- **Location.** This option sets your Mac to connect to different networks in different places. You probably will never use this option unless you take your Mac mini to the office—but even then, the system is usually able to connect itself to the network without user intervention.

- **Recent Items.** This option provides an easy way to access the applications, documents, and servers you've been using lately.

- **Force Quit.** Choose this option if an application hangs (yes, it sometimes happens) and you need to shut it down forcibly.

- **Sleep, Restart, Shut Down, Log Out.** These choices do what the names suggest.

Finder

The Finder is the application used to view the contents of folders and your hard drive. If you have no application on the screen, you will be in the Finder. If you have an application on the screen and click outside it, you will be in the Finder (**Figure 8.4**). You use the Finder to navigate the Mac OS X file system.

Windows also has an application, called Windows Explorer, that is much like the Mac OS X Finder. You open Windows Explorer by clicking a drive or folder, the same action that opens the Finder on a Mac.

In explaining the Finder, I'll also talk about how the menu bar at the top of the desktop works. The first option on the menu bar (just to the right of the Apple menu) is always the application you are presently running (Finder, Word, Mail, and so on—in the figure, it's the Finder). The rest of the left side of the menu bar changes to reflect the options for the application that is running.

The Finder also provides views of your hard drive's contents. At the left of a Finder window is the Sidebar. Click the hard drive's icon in the Sidebar to open the Finder's view of the drive. There are three views: Icons (**Figure 8.5**), List (**Figure 8.6**), and Columns (**Figure 8.7**). You can switch among views by clicking one of the three view buttons in a Finder window's toolbar (notice how the buttons light up). Note the browser-like Forward and Back buttons at the far left.

tip You can also change the view by selecting As Icons, As List, or As Columns from the View menu.

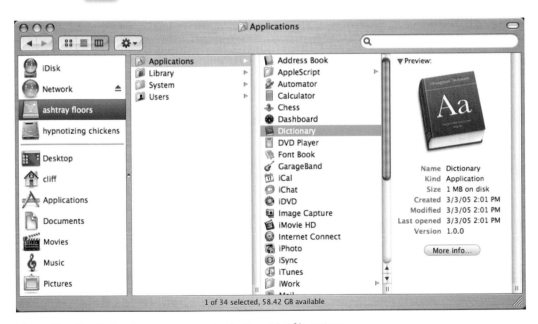

Figure 8.4 The Finder gives users access to the Mac OS X file system.

Forward
Back

Icons view
List view
Columns view

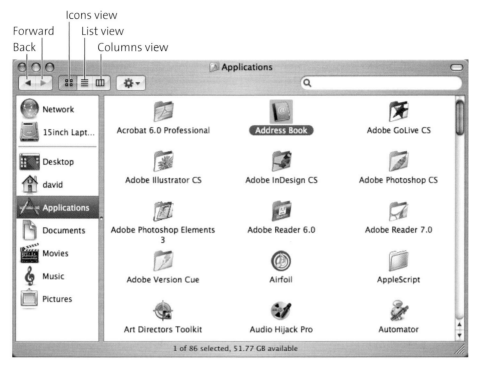

Figure 8.5 The Icons view of the files stored on this Macintosh.

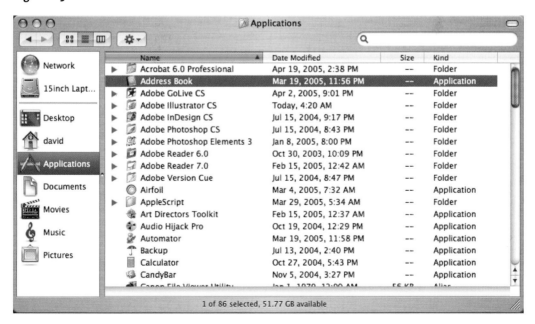

Figure 8.6 List view.

Note that Mac OS X organizes your applications, documents, and so on in their own folders, which you can select in the Sidebar of a Finder window or by navigating to them in the Finder itself. The folders in the Sidebar are open to all users and are where most applications will (and should) be kept. But each user also has a set of private folders of his or her own—see "Home Folder" later in this chapter for details.

If you don't like the arrangement of the icons on your Desktop or in any view, you can use the View menu to rearrange them (**Figure 8.8**).

Figure 8.7 Columns view.

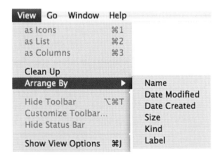

Figure 8.8 It's unavoidable: Your Mac mini's Desktop and folders will become jumbled. The View menu allows you to clean up the placement and choose the order in which icons are presented.

Menu Bar

In discussing the Desktop and Finder, I've already talked about some of the choices on the top menu bar. When you're in the Finder, the left side of the menu bar (**Figure 8.9**) includes the items already discussed—the Apple menu and Finder menu—plus the File, Edit, View, Go, Window, and Help menus. The Go menu provides another way to navigate the file system and has many of the same options found on the left side of Finder windows. The Connect to Server option is not as easy to use as the Network icon in the Sidebar of a Finder window as a means of finding and connecting to networked computers. The other menus work pretty much like their Windows counterparts.

tip Apple has done a very good job of building into its operating system and applications help that is actually helpful. Use it with confidence. Help is most useful if you are connected to the Internet as much additional information is available from Apple online.

The right side of the menu bar (**Figure 8.10**) provides some interesting options. Clicking any of these icons allows you to change the settings controlled by the icon.

Figure 8.9 The left side of the menu bar that appears at the top of the Mac OS X Tiger Desktop.

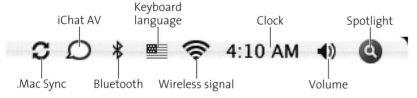

Figure 8.10 The right side of the Mac OS X Tiger menu bar. Click the icons to control the settings.

Here are what the icons indicate:

- **.Mac Sync.** The circle formed by arrows controls .Mac Sync, which is useful mainly if you have more than one Mac. It's discussed in Chapters 7 and 9. This is a cool feature, introduced with Mac OS X Tiger, but not one that many Mac mini–only customers will use.

- **iChat AV.** The iChat AV bubble icon lights when the iChat AV application is active, as shown in Figure 8.10.

- **Bluetooth.** If you buy your Mac mini with the Bluetooth option, you will see the Bluetooth icon. I have turned on Bluetooth just for this screen shot, so the icon isn't dimmed, as it would normally be.

- **Keyboard language.** The Mac comes preconfigured for use all over the world, and you can select keyboards (via the International System Preferences pane) for many languages. The U.S. flag icon shows that I have set my computer to offer other choices. Clicking the flag allows my wife to choose a Swedish flag, allowing her to use a keyboard set up for her native tongue. Unless you've set your computer to display an alternate choice, you won't see the flag icon.

- **Wireless signal.** The radio waves icon, with all the semicircles lighted, shows that I am using an AirPort Extreme wireless card and it is receiving an excellent signal. Fewer lighted semicircles indicate a weaker signal.

- **Clock.** Your Mac mini will automatically set itself to the correct time using a timeserver linked to an atomic clock.

- **Volume.** The two semicircles at the right of the speaker show that my speaker is set to a medium volume.

- **Spotlight.** The magnifying glass icon controls Spotlight, Mac OS X Tiger's powerful search feature. You'll learn more about Spotlight in the next section.

Spotlight

A new feature of Mac OS X Tiger, Spotlight is a search mechanism capable of finding just about anything anywhere on your Mac mini— and doing the job quickly. Clicking the blue magnifying glass icon opens a box where you can type your search terms. As Spotlight finds items, the results box opens (**Figure 8.11**).

Figure 8.11

Spotlight searches your hard disk and displays results from documents, PDF files, e-mail, contacts, folders, events and to-do lists, images— essentially, any file on your system. It can even find the names of artists and other information inside music and photo files. Here, the results box shows the items that a search on the word *fish* yielded.

The Spotlight System Preferences pane (**Figure 8.12**) allows you to choose the range of items searched.

Spotlight is a great new feature and one you will use often. You can also access it from Mail and other applications where you see the magnifying glass icon and a search field. In these cases, the search is limited to the application in use. One exception: The search field in the Safari browser initiates a Google search.

Apple is very proud of Spotlight, comparing it to features Microsoft has announced for versions of its operating systems not due for release until 2007 and beyond.

Mac OS X Tiger also lets you create Smart Folders (**Figure 8.13**). These folders contain the results of Spotlight searches and are constantly updated as you create new files or information changes. Smart Folders are an extension of the Smart Playlist concept first introduced in iTunes. Smart Folders are available from the Finder (on the File menu, choose Smart Folder) as well as in Mail and Address Book.

Here's an example: I want to create a Smart Folder to keep track of items related to Judy Ziajka, who copyedited this book. We traded a tremendous amount of e-mail and files. Using her last name as the search term for the folder (using the Contents search option), the Smart Folder finds every file that includes her last name. Every time I open the folder, the contents are automatically updated.

I also have a Smart Folder for mail we've exchanged. However, opening Spotlight (the blue magnifying glass icon) provides more comprehensive search results than Smart Folder does.

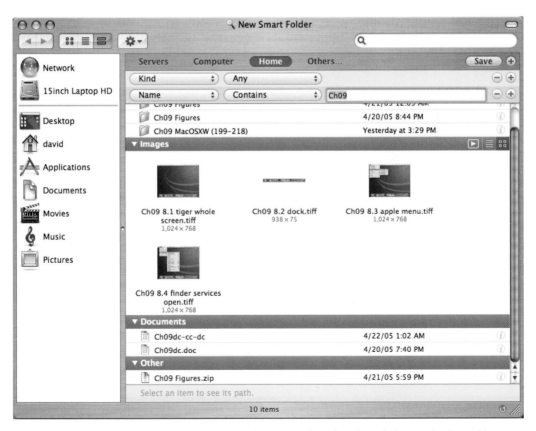

Figure 8.13 Each Smart Folder holds the results of a constantly updated Spotlight search of your files.

Dashboard

Dashboard, accessible from the Dock (it's the gauge icon on the left), opens a collection of small programs, which Apple calls widgets. These appear on a transparent screen layer placed over your Desktop so you can access them quickly. Notice how the layer darkens the screen (**Figure 8.14**).

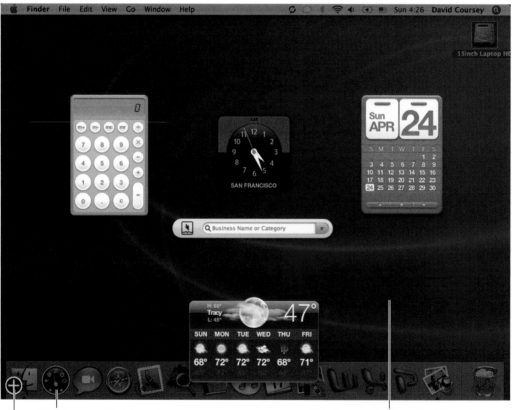

Click to open Dashboard   Click Desktop to close Dashboard

Click to open
widgets collection

Figure 8.14 Dashboard is a new Mac OS X Tiger feature that overlays small utility applications on the Desktop. The Calculator, World Clock, Calendar, Phone Book, and Weather widgets are shown here.

The widgets themselves are small, useful applications that provide tools, such as a calculator or clock, or that access information, such as a weather forecast. Widgets are also available from other companies, some for free and others for sale. Visit www.apple.com/downloads/macosx/dashboard/ to see a list of available widgets. (Remember: All URLs in this book can be found as links at www.peachpit.com/coursey.)

Widgets can be set up by rolling your cursor over them and then clicking the small italic letter *i* that lights up. Clicking an empty part of the screen (instead of a widget) closes the Dashboard.

You can select the individual widgets displayed on the Dashboard from a collection that appears when you click the circled plus (+) sign in the lower-left corner of the Dashboard screen. This opens the Widget bar, a panel of widgets at the bottom of the Dashboard (**Figure 8.15**). You can drag multiple copies of an item onto the Dashboard if, for example, you need multiple world clocks or weather forecasts.

To remove a widget from the Dashboard desktop, open the plus (+) sign menu, which opens the widget collection and also places an X on each desktop widget. Clicking the X of an individual widget removes it from the Dashboard desktop. Clicking the X on the widget panel closes the panel. Or you can hold down Option and place your cursor over a widget; click the X that appears in the top-left corner of the widget.

The Dashboard is another new feature of Mac OS X Tiger.

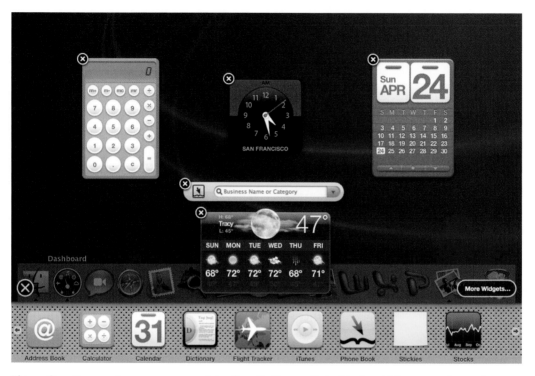

Figure 8.15 You can choose among a variety of applications, called widgets, which you can drag onto your Dashboard.

System Preferences

In Mac OS X, user settings are called preferences, as opposed to Microsoft Windows' control panels, settings, and options. A Mac application's preferences are available in its application menu—the Word menu for Microsoft Word, for example, or the iChat menu for iChat.

System Preferences, available from the Apple menu, provides access to Mac OS X setup and configuration options (**Figure 8.16**). This is a good place to go exploring to see what settings are available to you. Mac settings can be changed easily if you make a mistake.

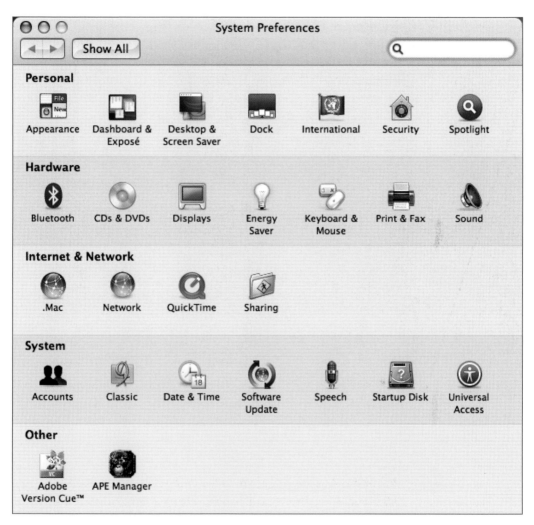

Figure 8.16 System Preferences, available from the Apple menu, allow you to change many Mac OS X settings.

Home Folder

Every Mac OS X user gets his or her own secure folder, not accessible to other users (unless you give them your password; **Figure 8.17**). However, an administrator can access home folders if necessary. The files in these folders are visible only when the named user is logged on.

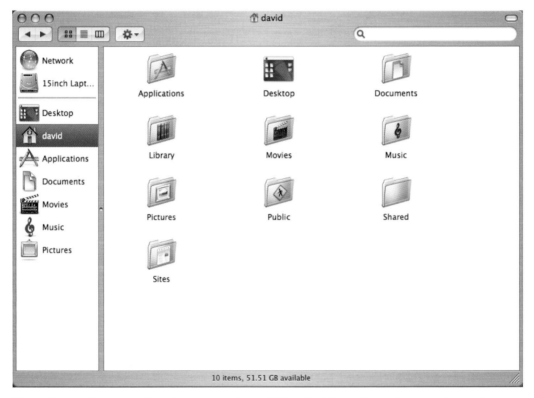

Figure 8.17 Each user gets his or her very own home folder, which bears the user's name. The user's personal files are kept in the home folder.

Parental Controls

Mac OS X Tiger offers a fairly comprehensive set of parental controls that can be used to limit what children (or anyone) can do on the Internet and on the Mac mini itself. To use these controls, you need to assign each user his or her own account, using the Accounts pane in System Preferences (Apple menu > System Preferences). For more about this feature, see Chapter 7.

More Help

So there you have a quick sightseeing tour of Mac OS X Tiger, the most advanced operating system available on a personal computer. If you spend an hour or two exploring on your own, I am confident you will get the hang of things.

But if you run into problems, the Apple Help system and Apple Support Web site have a wealth of information available. If you want to invest in a book, I am pleased to recommend these titles by my fellow Peachpit authors:

Mac OS X 10.4 Tiger: Visual QuickStart Guide, by Maria Langer; *Mac OS X 10.4 Tiger: Peachpit Learning Series* and *The Robin Williams Mac OS X Book, Tiger Edition,* both by Robin Williams; and *Getting Started with Your Mac and Mac OS X Tiger: Peachpit Learning Series,* by Scott Kelby.

Also, in my last book, I wrote a long chapter intended to help Windows users migrate to Mac. It's for an earlier version of Mac OS X, but most of the information still applies. I've turned the chapter into a PDF file, and it is available upon request. Visit www.peachpit.com/coursey for details.

9

Applications for the Mac mini

As you start to use the Mac mini, you may find that it comes with all the software you need: from an easy-to-use e-mail application and instant-messaging software to video-editing and DVD-creation tools and more. And if you need or just miss Microsoft Office, you'll find that the suite runs just fine on Mac OS X, too.

As you read this chapter, you will learn:

- About the great software that Apple includes with your Mac mini.

- How Microsoft Office on the Mac compares to the Windows version.

- About the .Mac service and whether you need it.

- About using your Mac mini to create a home media center.

Your Mac mini comes with an excellent collection of software—in fact, you may never need or want to buy anything else. In this chapter I discuss this free software, along with other software you may want to invest in. I will also use this chapter to answer some common questions about Mac applications.

At the end of this chapter, you'll learn how you can use the Mac mini as a media center for home entertainment.

Introducing Your Free Software

Here's a list of the software that comes with every Mac mini, usually preloaded on the hard disk.

Mail. An e-mail client program that will work with your POP, IMAP, or Microsoft Exchange–based e-mail (**Figure 9.1**). It also works with .Mac e-mail accounts. It does not include a calendar but is tightly linked to the Mac OS X Address Book. This is a very fine mail client, and the Spotlight search feature makes finding your messages easy.

Figure 9.1

The Apple Mail client, included with Mac OS X, is evolving to become a very fine product. Here you see my inbox, which includes mail from my Exchange server and .Mac account.

iChat AV. This is an instant messaging and conferencing application that connects .Mac, America Online, and Jabber users (**Figure 9.2**). You can conduct multiperson text, audio, and video conferences. For video conferences, you can use Apple's iSight camera or a Web cam from Logitech or another vendor.

Figure 9.2

iChat AV. The multilayered camera icon near my name indicates that I can conduct video chats with up to three other people at once (or audio chats with nine other people simultaneously). Since my friends lack such an icon, they can talk to only one person at a time. The handset next to Elionora's name indicates that my wife can audio chat. The red squiggles under the text show my spelling errors. They can be fixed by right-clicking or Control-clicking the word and selecting a spelling option from the pop-up menu.

Safari RSS. Microsoft has left the Mac browser business, and Apple has taken over. Safari (**Figure 9.3**) is a good browser, with a tabbed interface, and includes an RSS (short for Really Simple Syndication) reader for use with any Web site that employs RSS to distribute news and articles (sites that use RSS range from small Web logs to www.nytimes.com and, of course, www.apple.com).

Figure 9.3

Safari is to Mac OS X what Internet Explorer is to Windows (since there isn't an IE for Mac anymore). It's attractive and has among its features a tabbed interface, RSS news feed support, and a pop-up blocker.

Sherlock. An information access program, Sherlock (**Figure 9.4**) allows you to search the Web, find local movie schedules, browse an electronic yellow pages, find items on eBay, gather airline flight information, and look up words in a dictionary and translate them into other languages. It also provides an interface for the AppleCare help system. Some Sherlock features overlap widgets provided with the Mac OS X Tiger Dashboard.

Figure 9.4

Sherlock provides access to a variety of online information. Here are the available channels.

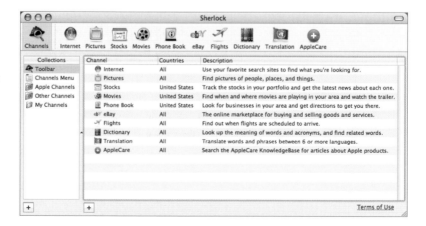

Address Book. This simple but powerful application ties into Mac OS X Mail and other Mac OS X applications (**Figure 9.5**). It does not provide as much information about a particular person as Microsoft Exchange or its Mac counterpart, Entourage, can. But if you don't need the Microsoft applications, you should give Address Book serious consideration. If you are a member of .Mac, you can share the contents of your Address Book with other .Mac members.

Figure 9.5
Here's my card from my own Address Book.

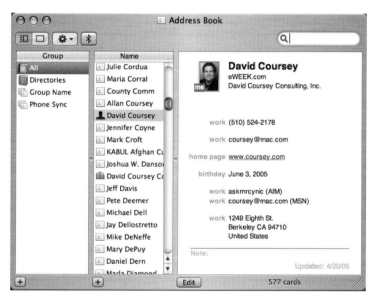

QuickTime. QuickTime is many things, including a player for Apple's video format (**Figure 9.6**).

iSync. Use iSync to synchronize information on your Mac mini with other devices, including cell phones and Palm OS devices. With Mac OS X Tiger, application synchronization across multiple Macintosh computers is now handled by .Mac, which requires a $99 annual membership.

iCal. This program provides a nice calendar that you can share with other Mac users (**Figure 9.7**). As with Mail and Address Book, I urge you to give iCal a chance before deciding you need something else.

Figure 9.6

QuickTime is a powerful Apple tool for creating, delivering, and playing media. Here the player appears in a Web page, showing a trailer for a motion picture.

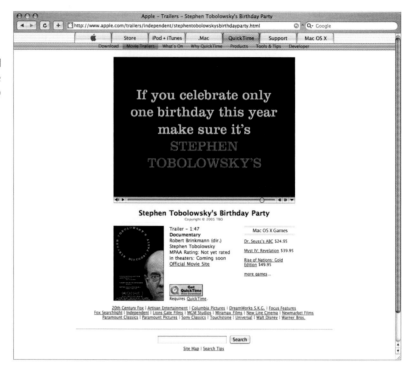

Figure 9.7

One of the perks of being a Peachpit author is lunches with your editor at a nice Mexican place near the office.

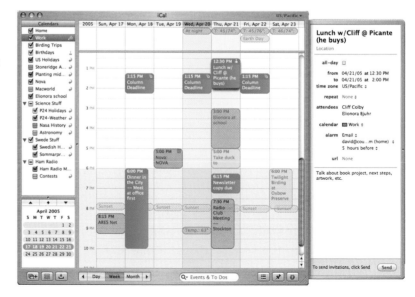

iLife '05 (includes iTunes, iPhoto, iMovie, iDVD, and GarageBand). This is Apple's creativity suite for home and small business users. Each of these programs is a real winner, and you would spend several hundred dollars if you purchased roughly equivalent programs for a Windows machine. iLife should be reason enough for many people to buy a Mac system. The programs are discussed individually later in this chapter.

How the iApps Came to Be

Everyone knows that software sells hardware. The best way to kill an operating system or a hardware platform is to starve it to death: Cut off the flow of new software, and sooner or later the platform goes away.

The software business has been pretty rough for the past decade or so as Microsoft has wiped out competitor after competitor. Many of these companies used to publish Mac applications, but the combination of Microsoft predation and Apple's declining market share led to a situation where Apple had to take matters into its own hands.

We should all face such misfortune, as Apple has countered this adversity with a bravura set of applications of its own creation. This is software that literally sells hardware—stand around an Apple Store for an hour or two, and you'll see it happen (if it hasn't already happened to you, that is).

Initially dubbed the iApps (after the original iMac), these programs include iTunes, iPhoto, iDVD, iMovie, iChat, iCal, and iSync. These applications are good, simple, and approachable enough that people are willing to buy Mac hardware because it's the only place you can find them.

All of these programs are included with the Mac mini for free. Apple also sells some of them in a suite called iLife, which offers iPhoto, iMovie, iTunes, iDVD, and GarageBand. The other iApps come with every Mac along with the operating system. A second collection of iApps comes in the $79 iWork suite, which includes Pages and Keynote.

The iApps are excellent applications—the sort of things Windows users pay money for but Mac users get for free. Whole books have been written about each of them, so I won't explain them in too much detail. But I do want to give you a taste of what each iApp looks like and what it does, and why the iApps may, all by themselves, be a good enough reason to get a Mac.

AppleWorks. This is not the greatest program in the universe, but it provides as much word processing, spreadsheet, and other Office-type functionality as you may need (**Figure 9.8**). Or perhaps you need the real Microsoft Office 2004 for Mac, discussed later in this chapter.

Figure 9.8

AppleWorks includes a simple database that looks very much like FileMaker, which Apple sells as a full-featured stand-alone product.

Quicken 2005 for Mac. This version of Quicken is somewhat behind the version currently available for Windows. But it also doesn't suffer the bloat of its counterpart, as feature after feature have been added to the Windows release (**Figure 9.9**).

Nanosaur 2 and **Marble Blast Gold.** All you need to know about these programs is that they are games.

Figure 9.9

Quicken 2005 brings financial management to the Mac mini desktop (and pretty much takes it over).

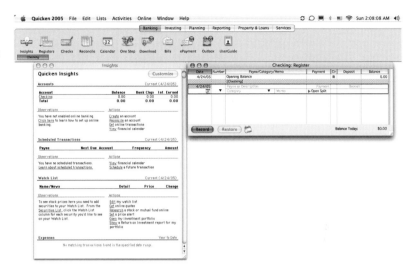

Sharing Your Life with a Mac mini and a Windows PC

In my previous book, *Mac OS X for Windows Users: A Switchers' Guide*, I was talking to people who were, ostensibly, trading in their Windows machine for a Mac. With the arrival of the Mac mini, users can easily keep their Windows PCs close at hand. And that raises some important questions that this section will attempt to answer about how to work with both Mac and Windows systems on your desk.

If I have a Mac mini, what should I use my Windows machine for?

As someone who periodically moves from Mac to PC and back, I know how hard living a dual life can be. How many address books, calendars, and mail clients can a person use at once, particularly when iCal still isn't Microsoft Exchange friendly in terms of sharing entries?

Here are some options:

Keep your Windows life intact and use the Mac mini for things Apple does best. That means you use the iLife applications but don't concern yourself with reading your mail, keeping your calendar, or maintaining your address book on the Mac mini.

Move your life to the iApps. If you don't need to talk to a Microsoft Exchange server at work, then Mail, Address Book, and iCal are probably better than what you are using today. In this case, move the information in these applications over to your Mac mini and save the PC for programs that aren't available for Mac or that you don't want to invest in. You can, for example, use Word and Excel on your Windows system regardless of the other Mac applications you use.

Move your life to Microsoft on the Mac. There are many, myself included, who believe that the Mac version of Microsoft Office is at least as good—even better—than the Windows version. Like the Windows version, Microsoft Office 2004 for Mac is available in a multiuser student package for less than $150. Office files can easily be moved from Mac to PC and back, and file compatibility is as close to 100 percent as I can measure. More on Office for the Mac later in this section.

Should I be concerned because there aren't as many applications for Mac OS as there are for Windows?

I'm betting that there will always be some programs that you use that aren't available for Macintosh. I have a handful of these, and being able to easily move from Mac to Windows with a KVM switch makes it really convenient to use either platform. I move files back and forth all day with no problems. But suppose you decide you love your Mac mini so much that you'd like to forget the PC entirely?

I think most people will do fine with the number and variety of applications available for Macintosh, as long as they don't need highly specialized business or leisure software.

Windows is the default platform for software developers, and many applications will never be developed for Macintosh. I am thinking particularly of games, a category where Apple lags way behind Microsoft. Of course, if you want games, I recommend a game console over a PC anyway.

When new devices are released, such as the Sprint PCS Vision wireless data modem card I'm using in my Windows XP laptop, they rarely include Mac drivers. The same goes for some of my ham radio and all my search-and-rescue software.

There also isn't a really great low-end Web-page–building package for Mac OS X, nor is there any really good mapping software. Freeway Express is a good, low-end Mac tool for Web creation, but I don't like it as much as Microsoft FrontPage, which I continue to use on the Windows machine. As for mapping, Mac users go online for maps and directions.

How does the Mac version of Microsoft Office compare with the Windows version?

The Mac version of Office compares quite favorably to the Windows version—and some Windows users actually believe that Office for Mac is a better product. The important thing to know is that Microsoft claims 100 percent file compatibility, and so far, I haven't been able to prove the company wrong. That means you can start a document on one platform, move it to the other for editing, and send it back without breaking anything (**Figure 9.10**).

Figure 9.10

Here is what a chapter of this book looked like in Microsoft Word on my Mac mini.

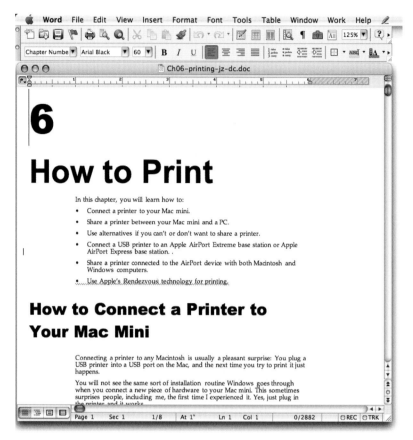

You should not confuse file compatibility with feature-set compatibility. Many features in Office for Windows are not in Office for Mac, and a few in Office for Mac aren't in the Windows version (**Figure 9.11**). I have been trying to find a list of these differences, but Microsoft says it doesn't have one. That sounds odd to me, but considering that the programs are built in different states (Washington for Windows and California for Mac) by different groups of developers who only sort of seem to talk to one another, perhaps it isn't surprising.

Figure 9.11

The Formatting Palette is a feature exclusive to the Mac version of Microsoft Word. It is an alternative to menu bars.

The good news is that I've yet to find anything I need to do that Office for Mac can't handle. It doesn't have all the gewgaws that have become part of the Office for Windows user interface, and it looks quite different. But when I am using Office for Mac, I really don't feel a major difference. I switch back and forth between the two all the time, and it's never been a problem. But if there are some obscure features that you use in Office for Windows, I would advise that you to verify that they are in the Mac version before you invest. An easy way to do this is to visit an Apple Store or other Mac reseller and see if you can play with a copy of Office on one of the store's machines. You can also download a "test drive" of Office for Mac from Microsoft's Mactopia site (www.microsoft.com/mac).

The bottom line: Office for Mac and Office for Windows look different but work very much the same.

So there are Office programs that aren't available for the Mac?

Office for Mac includes Word, Excel, PowerPoint, and a program you may never have heard of called Entourage, which handles e-mail, calendaring, and task management and synchronizes with Palm PDAs (**Figures 9.12** and **9.13**). It does not include FrontPage or Access. There is no Outlook for Mac OS X, nor are there programs such as Visio, which I have often heard requested by Mac users.

Figure 9.12

This is a view of a simple calendar in Microsoft Entourage, with a notification that popped up on the screen.

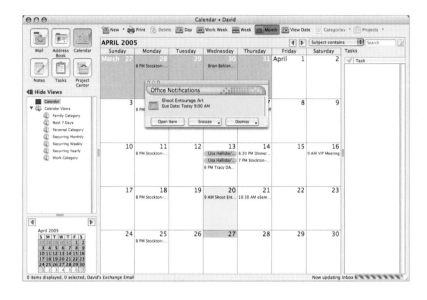

Figure 9.13

Here's what the Entourage inbox looks like when filled with messages from an Exchange server.

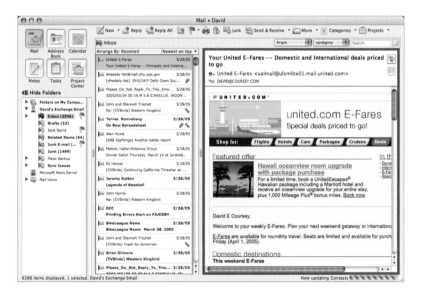

tip

There are charting programs for Mac OS X that the Visio user can adapt to, such as Blacksmith's Chartsmith, Computer Systems Odessa's ConceptDraw, and the Omni Group's OmniGraffle.

What do I use to replace Access?

If you are already a big Access user, I am not sure anything can replace it. But if you want to know what databases are available for Mac, there are a couple—but everyone I know uses FileMaker Pro.

FileMaker Pro is an excellent product, and as it has grown and changed, it hasn't disappointed me. The FileMaker line includes a number of products, such as pro, server, developer, and mobile versions.

Rather than do a not-very-good job of explaining FileMaker here, I'd rather you visit its Web site (www.filemaker.com), take a look around, and download the trial software. This will give you a great deal of insight into a very useful and usable database.

So I will leave it at this: FileMaker has my highest recommendation (**Figure 9.14**). Access never will.

Figure 9.14

FileMaker Pro, an Apple product, is the "standard" database for the Mac community and also runs on Windows systems.

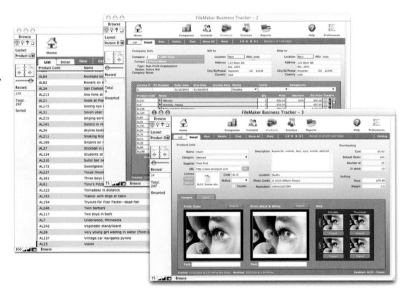

Why no Outlook for Mac?

Actually, there used to be a Mac version of Outlook, just as there was—a long time ago—a Mac version of FrontPage. My belief is that Microsoft is doing this in an attempt to keep Macintosh out of corporate accounts. Microsoft currently provides no method for accessing the full features of an Exchange server from Mac OS X client software.

How do I access my company's Exchange server from my Mac?

If you want to access your company's Exchange server from your Mac mini, you have several options, most of which require a little cooperation from your company's mail administrator.

Microsoft Entourage offers good, but not great, Exchange support. It does not, for example, store your tasks and notes on the server. I have lots of notes in Exchange, so this is a problem for me. Entourage does, however, use the contact list and calendar from the Exchange server, and those, along with mail, provide all the compatibility many people need.

Mac OS X Mail will happily download mail from your Exchange server and use it for sending your outbound mail. iCal will not link to an Exchange server, and Address Book claims to, but I've never been able to make it work (although one of my editors says he has).

My recommendation is that you download the trial version of Office for Mac and see if it does what you want. Setup is easy. Likewise, try Mac OS X's Mail client to see how you like it.

Another option is to ask your Exchange server administrator if Outlook Web Access is available. This solution gives you access to your e-mail, contacts, and calendar from any Web browser. The caveat is that you have to be able to get to your server in the first place, and that may require a VPN (virtual private network) connection between your Mac and your company's firewall. Apple provides a VPN client as a standard feature, but it may not work with all firewalls. Some firewall companies, however, have built their own Mac OS X clients, and Apple continues to make improvements. I believe most users will find the Apple VPN client acceptable.

Which version do I need?

Microsoft makes Office for Macintosh available in three versions: Standard, Student and Teacher, and Professional. These carry list prices of $399, $149, and $499, respectively.

What's the difference?

Standard and Student and Teacher are alike, including Word, Excel, PowerPoint, and Entourage. Professional also includes Virtual PC software that lets a Mac emulate a PC and run Windows applications. Also, the Student and Teacher Edition provides three installation codes, compared to one for each of the others.

Obviously, Student and Teacher Edition is a much better deal. But to buy it you need to qualify as Microsoft outlines here:

To license Office 2004 for Mac Student and Teacher Edition, you must be a Qualified Educational User or the parent or guardian of a Qualified Educational User who is a minor. Qualified Educational Users include: Full- or part-time students; home-schooled students; full- or part-time faculty or staff of an accredited educational institution.

Suppose I don't want to use Microsoft Office?

If you don't want to use Office, consider the free AppleWorks suite that comes with the Mac mini. Most Macs come with AppleWorks already installed (**Figure 9.15**). This is a simple but quite good suite of applications that can read and write Office documents. They include most of the functionality most users need most of the time (**Figures 9.16** to **9.17**).

Figure 9.15

Before you automatically drop $$$ for Microsoft Office, consider AppleWorks. Here are what AppleWorks calls its Starting Points for projects.

Figure 9.16

Here's AppleWorks in word processing mode.

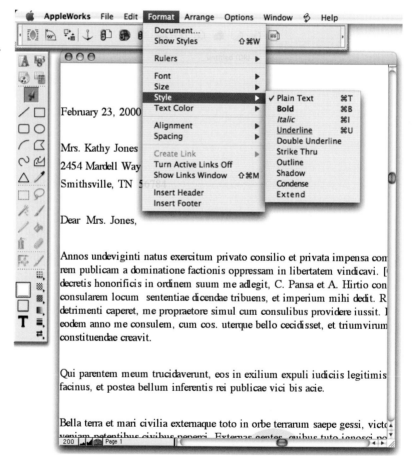

Figure 9.17

This is the AppleWorks spreadsheet, which you aren't likely to confuse with Excel. I have entered a few numbers and turned them into a very simple chart.

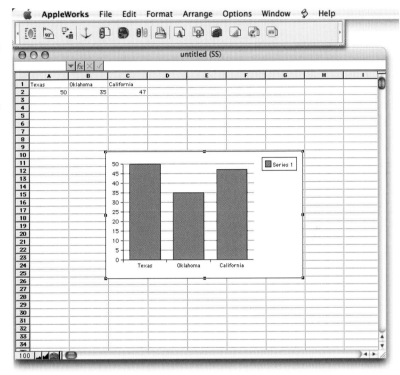

I won't lie to you: AppleWorks isn't Office, but it's very useful on its own terms and may be all you need. Read more about it later in this chapter. And if all you need is a word processor or a presentation application, you should also consider Apple's Pages and Keynote software, which make up the $79 iWork package.

What about the free Office software I've heard about?

I have occasionally played with various open-source or freeware programs that claim to compete with Microsoft Office. I cannot recommend any of them.

Software for Creativity

The iDVD, iMovie, and iPhoto applications (all part of the iLife suite) are designed to help you organize, edit, and distribute your digital photos and movies.

iMovie HD and iDVD

Having neither children nor an exhibitionistic streak, I am not in the target audience for iMovie and iDVD. As you've probably guessed, iMovie is for editing movies downloaded from your digital video camera, and iDVD is for creating DVDs, complete with menus and graphics.

Both are excellent programs, and Mac mini users get them for free. Both are entry-level versions of fuller, professional-level programs—Final Cut Pro and DVD Studio Pro—that Apple sells to people who earn their living making movies and DVDs.

The first time I used iMovie, I shot some video at the going-away party for a co-worker as a demonstration; it took me about 30 minutes to feel comfortable with the program (**Figure 9.18**). There is no big manual for iMovie—just help files—because the program doesn't need one. It was only later that I discovered the tutorials at the iMovie Web site.

Figure 9.18

iMovie has a simple interface yet provides the novice videographer with much of the functionality of a professional software package. iMovie comes with a handful of effects, including the Ken Burns Effect (up there in the top-right corner), which lets you add a sense of motion to still images. (Courtesy Apple Computer)

Using a feature called Magic iMovie, you can have the program do the work of assembling a movie for you. The program will import and arrange your video on a timeline, creating a movie from start to finish. It can optionally add titles, transitions, chapter markers, and a soundtrack. When the movie is completed, the program can also automatically send it to iDVD.

The HD in the name stands for "high-definition," and the program supports HDV 720p and 1080i widescreen formats.

 If I were buying a Mac strictly for video editing or even with the intention of creating home movies on a regular basis, I'd buy an iMac or Power Mac rather than a Mac mini—not that the Mac mini can't do the work, but a faster processor and larger hard drive would be quite useful.

With a compatible FireWire digital video camera, getting video off the camera is plug-and-play simple—with iMovie able to fully control the camera. Editing is easy to learn, but making the proper artistic edits takes some skill and learning. Fortunately, television has made most of us fairly video literate, so it's easy to imitate something we've seen before. And iMovie includes a basket full of special effects.

iDVD, included with Macs that have a built-in DVD recorder (which Apple calls a SuperDrive), makes it pretty simple to put one or more movies, as well as slide shows, on a single DVD. iDVD creates the menu structure that's necessary for using the disc with a consumer DVD player. It's lots of fun to use (**Figure 9.19**).

Figure 9.19

This is iDVD, which lets you bring an extra bit of Hollywood to your home videos before you burn them to disc. Remember that you need a SuperDrive-equipped Mac mini to burn DVDs.

iPhoto

Here's a program that I think has been a tad overrated, mostly because of confusion over what it does.

If you always take perfect digital photographs—or are just too lazy to make them better—then iPhoto may be all the digital photography software you need. You can use it to import photos from your camera to your Mac, do some touch up, print the images, create Web pages, and assemble your photos into very cool books that Apple will have professionally printed for you (**Figure 9.20**). With iPhoto 5, Apple lowered the prices of the books and added new sizes, making them attractive as photographic scrapbooks or as gifts.

iPhoto 5 also has better image-enhancement capabilities than previous versions and supports RAW image formats, which some photographers will find useful.

None of those things are really what iPhoto is about, however; the heart and soul of iPhoto are its organizational capabilities. iPhoto is the best tool I know of to easily organize all those thousands—maybe tens of thousands—of images that quickly move from digital camera to hard drive (often never to be seen again).

Figure 9.20
Celebrate special occasions (or any time) with a photo book created from in iPhoto. You can use images you've sized and doctored in another program (such as Adobe Photoshop Elements).

With iPhoto, your entire photo collection, or whatever portion of it you want to see, is immediately available for viewing, using one of the sharpest visual interfaces I've ever seen (**Figure 9.21**).

Figure 9.21

This is a view of some small thumbnail images from my collection as shown in iPhoto.

Most digital photography programs make use of scaled-down *thumbnail* images so you can see a number of pictures on the screen at once. iPhoto, however, is the only program I've seen that makes it easy to zoom in and out, so you can quickly go from many images on your screen to just one, if that's all you want.

You use a slider to easily control the zooming and scroll bars to control your movement through your photo collection (**Figure 9.22**). This is about as easy as wading through a zillion digital images can be.

As I said, iPhoto is not the best choice for fixing problem photographs, although many will be perfectly happy with the program's features for retouching and enhancing photographs, especially with the recent improvements. This is especially the case when buying a better piece of software—I recommend Adobe Photoshop Elements 3.0—could set you back nearly $100, or more.

Figure 9.22
Move the slider at the bottom right, and the images go from teensy to a decent size. No, I am not crazy; there's a barn owl family living in that hole.

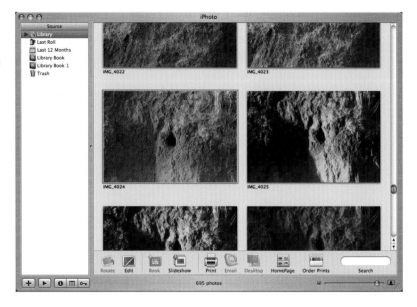

About the Macintosh "Sole Source"

One thing Windows users notice when they buy a Mac is that there is not as much software or as many accessories available for Macintosh as for their Windows PC. They also notice that in many cases there may be only one or two vendors competing for the Mac market.

Windows users see this as a reflection of Mac's small share of the total PC market, which is true enough. But Mac users actually consider this a feature rather than a problem.

How can this be?

In the Mac universe, there may exist only one of many items, but that one is likely to be pretty good. If you were to walk into a PC store and randomly grab a product and do the same in an Apple Store, you'd almost certainly find the Apple product easier to use and probably of better overall quality.

Macintosh users tend to be happy that limited selection generally means better products. And everyone ends up using the same things, creating a support network and making it much easier to find a helping hand when you need one.

For example, most amateur digital photographers who use Macs use iPhoto or Adobe Photoshop Elements 3. Both of these are great products. For Windows users, there are many more products to choose from.

The new version of Photoshop Elements includes organizational features that in some ways exceed iPhoto's capabilities. Maybe I'm vain, but I'd never show anyone a digital photo that hadn't been through Photoshop, and Photoshop Elements makes a large part of this powerful (and otherwise expensive) program available at a very decent price ($89). If you are serious about digital photography, take a look at the trial version that you can download at Adobe's Web site: www.adobe.com.

Software for Music

Your Mac mini includes two audio applications for creating and playing music: GarageBand and iTunes.

GarageBand

GarageBand (**Figure 9.23**) is an "honorary" iApp for home musicians, providing small-studio composition and multitrack recording features as part of the iLife package. Apple also sells Jam Packs of playable musical instruments and loops that can be used with GarageBand. Some of these are available free to .Mac members as well.

Figure 9.23

GarageBand looks very much like a high-end recording studio package. (Courtesy Apple Computer)

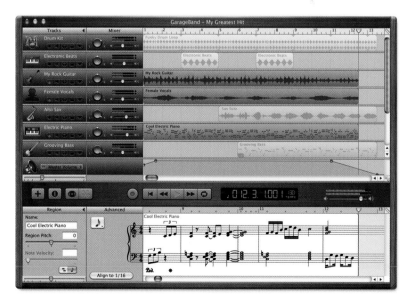

I have played with GarageBand enough to prove I am not a musician, but my musician friends say it's a serious tool for beginners. I like watching it create musical notation on the fly.

iTunes

When the first MP3 players came on the market, I sort of wondered what the fuss was about. Sure, you could carry music with you, if you call carrying an hour or two of tunes actually "carrying music." Hope that bike ride won't be a very long one, or else you'd better like those tunes a whole lot.

And yes, you could download the music you'd stolen over the Internet onto an MP3 player—in only slightly less time than it would take to play it. Okay, I exaggerate, but moving music to an MP3 player via USB cable is pretty slow.

Then along came Apple's iPod. The iPod—basically a multigigabyte hard drive with an operating system, a little processor, a headphone jack, a cute little dial for navigating through your music, and a FireWire or USB 2 port—is one of the coolest inventions I've seen.

Coupled with iTunes, the iPod can download a CD from a Mac or PC in about 10 seconds. With its large hard drive, you can literally carry thousands of songs in your pocket.

 I have a couple of iPods, one of which carries just my collection of old-time radio programs (visit www.otrftpserver.com for inexpensive downloads). Because a 30-minute program translates into only a 6 MB file, I am able to carry more than a *month's* worth of programs on one iPod. MP3 files and downloads have given new life to wonderful radio shows—*The Shadow*, *The Jack Benny Program*, *The Lone Ranger*, *Dragnet*, *Johnny Dollar*, and others.

iTunes is also the product that "saved" Apple and brought many Windows users into Apple Stores. Thanks to the Windows version of iTunes, iPods work for Microsoft users, too. But many of these people still end up in an Apple Store to buy their iPod or accessorize it. For some, the ultimate accessory is a Macintosh computer, which brings us to the Mac mini and this book.

If your music collection is large enough, it makes sense to buy a Mac mini just to warehouse it. With AirPort Extreme and an AirPort Express Base Station, you even have the ability to wirelessly deliver music from iTunes (Mac or Windows) to speakers around your home or office.

Since iTunes playlists can be shared—again between all computers on your network, Mac or Windows—I can be upstairs using a Mac laptop, open a playlist of music from the Mac mini downstairs, and listen to the music through the powered speakers of my Bose Wave Radio (**Figure 9.24**).

The iTunes software lets you store information about your music, including a personal rating and how often you play a particular song. A Smart Playlist feature uses this information to create collections of, say, your 50 highest-rated songs, or the tunes you listen to most often, or music by a specific composer or from a specific year.

Dragging and dropping songs is not the only way to create a playlist. Smart Playlists significantly automates the process, even down to noticing new music that's added or statistics that change after the playlist is created. And iTunes has hooks into the other members of the iLife suite, so, for example, you can use music from your iTunes library in an iPhoto slideshow.

Figure 9.24

There is a lot going on here. I am viewing and playing a song from a music collection kept on another Mac. The music is being sent from a computer downstairs to speakers in a Bose Wave Radio in the bedroom that is connected to an AirPort Express Base Station. Yes, this is all wireless.

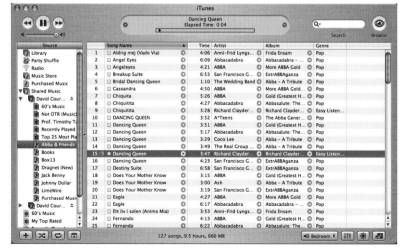

iTunes also has a feature that automatically adjusts the volume on your entire music collection, preventing one song from playing dramatically louder or softer than the others.

Audible.com's collection of downloadable books and other spoken content—such as Public Radio programs—is supported by iTunes and iPod as well. I used to carry books on my Pocket PC, but the iPod's much larger capacity means that I can both carry more books and download higher fidelity versions of the files.

The one thing I don't like about iTunes is that it's only an MP3 player for radio stations. That means iTunes will tune in to only Internet radio stations that broadcast an MP3 stream. Although streaming MP3 tends to be very high quality (high bandwidth, too), very few stations broadcast in that format.

tip   **If you want to hear NPR on iTunes, click the Radio button in the Source window. In the Public section, look for the KCRW or WNYC feed in the radio stations list.**

For that reason, I find the iTunes' Internet radio tuner to be essentially useless, although in the bigger scheme of things, it's not all that important. RealNetworks' RealOne media player will tune in to all the Internet radio I care to listen to.

If you buy a Mac mini and don't already have an iPod, you should dig a little deeper and get one. But until you do, there are many enjoyable hours to be had using iTunes alone to rip songs from your CD collection, manage them on your Mac, and then burn them onto CDs you can use in the car or on a portable player.

Or you can visit the third leg of the iPod trinity, the iTunes Music Store, to download music to your heart's content (and wallet's detriment) for only 99 cents a song (**Figure 9.25**). You can't give this music to your friends, but you can play it on multiple Macs or iPods. And you can also pick and choose the music on a song-by-song basis, meaning that you don't have to buy an entire album just to get one song you like.

Figure 9.25

Apple's iTune's music store provides an excellent way to build a music collection. The 99-cents-a-song fee may seem expensive until you remember all the whole albums you used to purchase just to get one or two songs you actually wanted.

The combination of iPod, iTunes, and iTunes Music Store, for both Mac and Windows, is a stupendous achievement. The Mac mini enhances the trio further.

tip

There are many companies that make fine Macintosh accessories, many of them directed toward iPod, GarageBand, iChat, and digital photography users. Some of the best are made by Griffin Technology and Belkin Corp. Visit www.griffintechnology.com and www.belkin.com to see the latest.

Software for Organization, Communication, and Business

Your Mac mini includes these programs to help you work effectively and efficiently: Address Book, AppleWorks, iCal, iChat AV, iSync, iWork, Mail, Preview, Safari, and Sherlock. You may also want to consider a subscription to .Mac, which provides a number of utilities, including backup functions and an e-mail service.

Address Book

The Mac OS X Address Book is where you keep information about your contacts. It also can be synchronized with your PDA, iPod, and some wireless handsets that are Bluetooth enabled. Spotlight integrates with Address Book to make your contact information easily searchable.

Address Book is an example of Mac OS X's doing the right thing. The Address Book itself is functional and not nearly as overwhelming as the contact manager in Outlook can be (**Figure 9.26**).

Figure 9.26
Address Book won't store as many types of information as Microsoft Outlook. Here are the fields you can use in Address Book, which are quite enough for most people.

Click and hold the label to the left of an address, and you can select Map Of from a pop-up menu to take you to a map showing its location. Click and hold the label to the left of a phone number, and you can choose an option to display the number very large across the middle of the screen—just the thing when you have to walk over to the fax machine.

Address Book also works with iSync, .Mac Sync, and Bluetooth-enabled (meaning expensive) cellular telephones.

Address Book searching is fast and full-text by default.

AppleWorks

AppleWorks (see Figures 9.15, 9.16, and 9.17) is a six-function basic productivity suite that includes word-processing, spreadsheet, painting, drawing, presentation, and database functionality. It also knows how to read and write Word and Excel documents.

I will not try to convince you that AppleWorks does everything Office does—it doesn't. But I would challenge you to spend a week or two with your new Mac mini and see if the combination of AppleWorks, iCal, Address Book, iSync, Safari, and Mac OS X Mail doesn't meet most of your software needs.

If you then do decide you need full-bore Office for Mac, go right ahead. But be sure you buy the student edition, if you qualify.

Most people buy way more software than they need because the software companies keep telling them that they need more and more features. Sure, there are new bells and whistles in new software, and I love many of them, but before you spend money for features you don't need, give AppleWorks a chance.

However, in the interest of full disclosure, every word of this book—and my previous one—was written in Microsoft Word.

iCal

iCal is a personal calendar application that does a very nice job of helping you manage your time. Apple's description of it as "elegant" is appropriate, and comparing iCal to Microsoft Outlook offers an excellent example of the differences between Apple's way of thinking and Microsoft's.

iCal lets you create separate color-coded calendars for your work, home, school, or other activities (**Figure 9.27**). You can view all these calendars at once in a single day-at-a-glance, week-at-a-glance, or month-at-a-glance window.

You can use iCal to remind you of appointments, watch approaching deadlines, send and receive e-mail notifications, set alarms, and create and prioritize to-do lists associated with each calendar.

Figure 9.27

iCal is a very functional calendaring program that allows you to store different parts of your life in different calendars (as shown at the left side of the screen). You can also share calendars and subscribe to other people's calendars, including several you see here. The daily sunset time appears courtesy of a shared calendar.

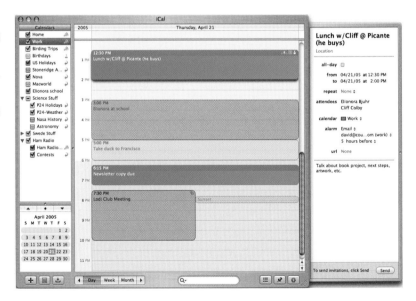

You can quickly view or hide your various calendars, making it easy to see and print calendars for specific parts of your life. By turning off your calendars for home events while you're working, for example, you can focus on just those events that matter at the time. Turn on the calendars for all events, and you can easily spot conflicts and empty spaces in your schedule.

You can share iCal calendars online, using Publish from iCal's Calendar menu. You must be a .Mac member to do this unless you have a Web server configured to serve the calendar, which seems much more difficult than being a .Mac member.

Publishing a calendar gives others access to your events or to public calendars (sporting events, club meetings, and so on) that you create. Mac users subscribe to published calendars via .Mac. Windows users can view (but not subscribe to) calendars by viewing a page on the creator's .Mac Web site. When you upload an iCal calendar to your .Mac account, you're provided a URL on your .Mac Web site where the calendar can been seen, and you can also create an e-mail message so you can tell friends.

Apple offers a bunch of its own iCal calendars you can subscribe to. While exploring the Apple Web site, I subscribed to public calendars for U.S. holidays, Swedish holidays, and events at my local Apple Store.

iCal makes it easy to remind yourself of important events. Besides screen pop-ups and sounds, iCal can send e-mail messages at a specified interval before an event. These can go to any device with an e-mail address, such as a pager or cell phone.

Should You Subscribe to .Mac?

One question you will doubtless be confronted with is whether to spend $99 a year for a .Mac subscription (or $179 for a five-user family pack). Apple offers a trial membership in the hopes that you'll become a paying member when the free trial ends. The question is: Is .Mac a good deal?

Here's what the subscription buys, in my perceived order of value to Mac mini customers:

Backup

A .Mac membership gets you access to Backup, a program that allows you to automatically copy specific types of files to your iDisk. I have mine set to run every day at 2 A.M. I also use Backup to make a safe copy of my information on DVDs and external hard drives.

Backup does not make an image of your Mac mini than can be used to completely re-create your hard drive. If you suffer a major crash, you will have to reinstall the operating system and applications before using Backup to restore your files. Read more in Chapter 7.

iDisk

Your account includes 250 MB of space on Apple's servers—and you can purchase more. You can access files you store on your iDisk from almost any Windows or Mac machine with an Internet connection.

While writing this book, I always kept a copy of the book's files on my iDisk, just in case something bad happened to my computer or even to my whole house. I also occasionally use iDisk to send large files to friends, either because my ISP or theirs won't accept them. With iDisk, I can set up a user account for the friend if I want to protect the files from unauthorized eyes, or I can merely drop the file into my Public folder if I don't care who sees it. Either way, my friend uses a browser to download the files.

You can also access your iDisk from a Windows machine.

Of course, iDisk is typically too slow to use as though it were a local hard disk. For example, I accidentally started saving my book document files directly to iDisk. Processing was so slow that I thought that my computer had gotten sick before I realized my error. After that, I was careful to save only final copies or to drag and drop files to my iDisk.

Should You Subscribe to .Mac? *(continued)*

E-mail

Yes, you probably already have an e-mail account, but if you don't, .Mac offers a nice mail service, which gets you a mail address in the form of *username*@mac.com. Some people think that's pretty cool, and it is nice to have an e-mail address you don't have to change if you move to a different job or school. You can also check your .Mac e-mail through a Web browser and purchase additional mailboxes for others in your family (**Figure 9.28**). You still need an ISP.

Figure 9.28

The Mail client will download your .Mac inbox, or you can use a Web browser to see your mail from wherever you happen to be.

.Mac Sync

New in Mac OS X Tiger is the ability to synchronize your Mail rules and accounts, calendar, Address Book, passwords, Safari bookmarks, and other items among multiple Macintoshes (**Figure 9.29**). If you have only one Mac, it's still to good run .Mac Sync, just to keep a copy of this information available in case of a hard drive crash.

(continues on next page)

Should You Subscribe to .Mac? *(continued)*

Figure 9.29
In Mac OS X Tiger, .Mac gained the ability to synchronize information among different Macintosh computers. You'll love this if you have more than one Mac.

HomePage Web Publishing

If you want to create a simple Web site, perhaps to share photos and files, .Mac's HomePage makes the process pretty easy. Because .Mac throttles heavy usage, this isn't a good place to keep all those music files your friends want to download by the zillions. But it integrates nicely with iPhoto for building pages from your photographs and is generally easy to use.

What's the Answer?

If you are pretty sure (perhaps from your PC experience) that you won't make regular backups, then .Mac is easy insurance against some forms of catastrophe. If you don't have an e-mail account and think having a .Mac address is cool, there's another reason for using .Mac. I am fond of having a copy of my Address Book saved by the .Mac Sync feature. And HomePage and iPhoto do work nicely together.

Apple promotes .Mac as a set of "Internet essentials" for its customers. If you agree, then the price is reasonable enough. But if you use only a portion of .Mac, then you have to do the math and decide whether you get enough value to justify the price.

I used to be pretty down on .Mac, but the service has improved since its introduction a few years ago, and today I am able to recommend it to users who need what it offers. I think what I get from .Mac is worth the money.

iChat AV

The iChat instant-messaging (IM) and conferencing program is great, as far as it goes—which in the current release is pretty far, with multi-person audio and video conferencing. iChat was the first outside client software that AOL licensed to use its instant-messaging network. The AOL relationship gives iChat users immediate access to 150 million AOL Instant Messaging users as well as .Mac users.

tip

There are a number of cameras that work with iChat AV to provide video conferencing, including those from Logitech. But the best I've found, not surprisingly, is Apple's own iSight camera. It also happens to be, at $149, the most expensive.

Using a technology called Bonjour (formerly Rendezvous), you can see which people are available on your local network without even knowing their screen names. Although you may not want to type-talk to someone that close to you, it offers an excellent drag-and-drop way to send or receive files.

The first thing most people notice about iChat is that the chats look different than other chats. First, it's easy to use a picture in iChat—of yourself, perhaps—as an icon, and the dialog itself appears in thought bubbles that look like cartoons. If this bothers you, just turn off the bubbles by selecting View > Show as Text. You can also select the way that people are identified; the best way is to display names and maybe pictures, if you like.

tip

Don't use pictures alone, because people without pictures get generic icons, and you won't be able to tell who they are.

The program provides the usual font, color, and smiley options that allow you to make your messages either more personal or merely annoying, depending on the mood of the recipient. And there is also a chat-log feature, which may prove useful or incriminating, depending on your online habits.

iChat is integrated with the Mac OS X Address Book and Mail applications, so you don't have to endlessly retype contact information. The .Mac and AOL Instant Messaging (AIM) account names for your contacts are stored along with their e-mail addresses and other contact information. Adding someone to your Buddy List is as simple as dragging his or her Address Book entry to the Buddy List. Mac OS X Mail is also buddy-aware and gives you the opportunity to IM rather than reply to an e-mail if the sender is online when you are.

There are lots of instant-messaging clients in the world—including several for the Mac, such as Yahoo, MSN Messenger, and AOL Instant Messaging. iChat happens to be one of the nicer ones. Yahoo Messenger rates tops with the largest feature set, but iChat is the most fun to use. There is also a multiservice chat client called Fire that runs under Mac OS X.

iSync

With the introduction of Mac OS X Tiger, iSync has lost some importance. It used to be the only Apple-provided synchronization tool. Now, .Mac Sync has expanded the synchronization options.

This is another of those things Apple is doing that Microsoft should have done first. iSync keeps your contact and calendar information synchronized across multiple devices, including Palm OS–based personal digital assistants (PDAs), the address book and calendar on iPods, and a handful of Bluetooth-enabled cell phones.

Synchronizing a PDA, iPod, and phone using iSync is a one-button process. Setup is straightforward, as iSync looks for devices connected to your system and helpfully offers to connect them.

iWork

There are two programs that are not included with the Mac mini that deserve mention. They are Keynote and Pages, which together form a package called iWork.

Simply, Keynote is an excellent presentation program that creates much more interesting "slideware" than PowerPoint does (**Figure 9.30**). Of course, you need a Mac to show a Keynote presentation, so if all you have is a Mac mini, you probably won't be making a lot of presentations—though hauling the Mac mini is easier than transporting many laptops.

Figure 9.30
Keynote is what PowerPoint should be: classy. Keynote templates look great, and it's easy to add iPhotos, iMovies, and other media to them.

Pages is Apple's attempt at a word processor with strong page design features. It does not offer as many features at Microsoft Word, but it goes deep into those that make a printed page stand out (**Figure 9.31**). However, Pages is a new product and it shows, and I don't recommend that people purchase it until improvements are made. However, the iWork package costs $79, and Keynote alone is worth that.

Mail

I have always liked the Mac OS X Mail client, which is significantly improved with the addition of the Spotlight search feature and improved connectivity to Microsoft Exchange servers (**Figure 9.32**). The only thing I don't like is the inability to drag an e-mail message to iCal to create a calendar item.

Figure 9.31

The nicest thing I can say about Pages is it's a first-generation product that will improve over time. Today, it's filled with gorgeous templates that most users will find impossible to duplicate.

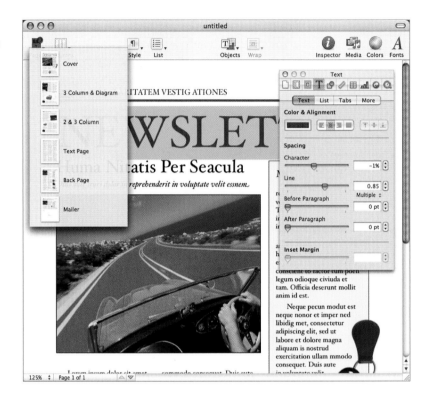

Figure 9.32

Here's my inbox in Apple's Mail program. This is a mix of Exchange and .Mac mail. Note the Smart Mailboxes that automatically gather messages to, from, or about specific people or about a topic or project of interest. The shading on three inbox items shows that they are related to the message I have selected.

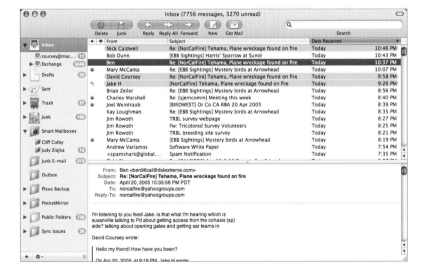

Mail has a very nice junk-mail filter, which you turn on from the preferences panel (**Figure 9.33**). It uses a technology called latent semantic analysis that allows the Mail program to do a better job of stopping spam than many other mail programs or spam filters.

Figure 9.33

This is the junk mail preferences pane in the Mac OS X Mail program.

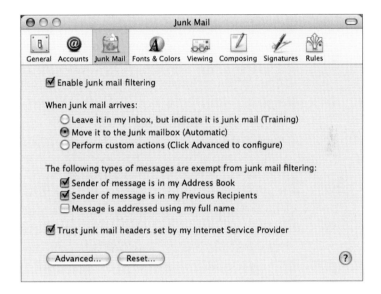

When you first use the junk-mail filter, set it to Training mode, in which it identifies junk mail, turning it an appropriate brown color, but still delivering it to your mailbox. Then, if you agree with the program's junk-mail determination, do nothing.

You will, however, find some messages that are junk that were missed, and some messages that aren't junk but were labeled that way. In each case, you simply click a button that toggles between Junk and Not Junk, enabling you to change the status of a message.

When you're satisfied that the junk filter understands what you think is and isn't junk, switch to Automatic mode, and the spam is automatically sent to the Junk folder, which is automatically emptied weekly.

At least that's how I set my Mail program to work. Every few days I look at the Junk folder to make sure nothing important got put there by mistake (very rare), and about twice a day I need to click the Junk button to handle a piece of spam that snuck through. Considering the amount of spam I get each day, I consider the ease of use and spam-fighting features of the Mail program to be remarkable.

Mail is capable of managing several POP, IMAP, .Mac, and Exchange e-mail accounts, enabling you to view them individually or in a single combined view. You can also create folders to store messages you need to hold on to. Any message from any mailbox can be dragged to any folder for storage. The program handles drag-and-drop attachments, displays photos in the message body (and can play a slideshow of attached photos), and uses the common Address Book available to all Mac OS X applications.

Preview

Mac OS X is unique in that it uses Adobe PostScript technology for its displays and printing. This means that every Print dialog allows you to create PDF documents, using the Adobe Acrobat PDF file format. There are Acrobat readers for almost all operating systems, including Mac, Windows, and Linux. That makes PDF a safe choice for sending files to people who might not have the application used to create a document.

Mac OS X uses an application called Preview to open PDF files for viewing. It allows users to copy text from PDF documents for use in other applications. Preview also displays some graphics formats.

Preview allows you to view and create comments in PDF documents, but is otherwise not as fully featured as the free Acrobat Reader program or the authoring software sold by Adobe Systems. Visit www.adobe.com.

Safari

Back in 1996, Apple released a Web browser called Cyberdog. Although those who used it loved it, Cyberdog never caught on, and Apple quietly put it on the shelf. The company, however, apparently never stopped dreaming of having its own browser, because Apple kicked off 2003 by releasing another Web browser. Called Safari, it employs a handful of clever features that make browsing the Internet a snap. For example, the application includes a Google search field right in its address bar. It also uses a smart tabbed interface and can display RSS newsfeeds from your favorite Web sites. It also includes a pop-up blocker and a private-browsing mode that lets you protect personal information.

Microsoft Internet Explorer is no longer being developed for Macintosh. There are, however, at least three alternative browsers—Firefox, from the Mozilla project; OmniWeb, from the Omni Group; and Opera, from Opera Software—that are available for Mac OS X.

Sherlock

Here's an application that I'd like to get excited about but haven't been able to. Why? Because Sherlock has been a heartbreaker, and I am not putting myself through that again.

The pitch goes like this: "Sherlock 3 displays custom information in a context-specific window so you can grasp the information you want quickly." That's what Apple says about Sherlock, which you might also think of as a particularly nifty Web-search utility (**Figure 9.34**).

Figure 9.34

Use Sherlock to do a search for *bats* (the flying mammal), and here's what you get.

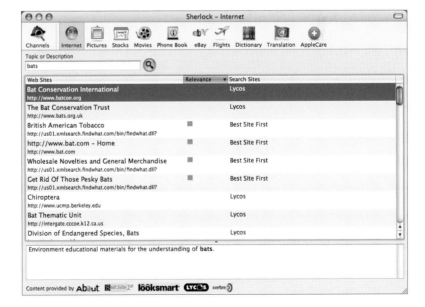

Included with Sherlock are channels dedicated to finding pictures; tracking stocks; getting movie listings; tracking flights; looking up words in a dictionary; letting your fingers do the walking in an online Yellow Pages; translating text to and from a variety of languages; getting support from Apple; and buying trash, trinkets, and treasures on eBay.

Type the name of a person in the Pictures channel, and you'll get a bunch of thumbnails, hopefully of the person you are looking for. (Google works better, by the way.)

The movie finder is very cool, if you like sitting in dark rooms with a few hundred other folks. You can search by movie title or theater. And it also shows movie trailers—a chance for Apple to show off QuickTime (**Figure 9.35**).

Figure 9.35

Here's what's showing at a local theater, courtesy of Sherlock's Movies channel.

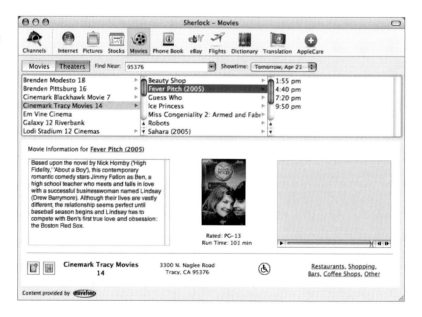

Because Sherlock is just a nice front end to other people's information, you're stuck if you don't like the services Apple has partnered with. One useful setting stores addresses you can use with the Yellow Pages feature to tell it where you are so it can find nearby stores (**Figure 9.36**).

Figure 9.36

I asked Sherlock to find the nearest Starbucks, and it produced a list, plus a map and directions. This is much more complete than what the Yellow Pages widget in Dashboard provided (no map, no directions).

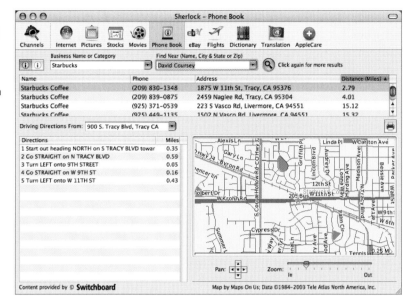

So why am I reserving a measure of affection? Well, there are the earlier versions, which never lived up to their promise. Here's another quote from Apple's description of Sherlock 3: "And you can look forward to asking Sherlock to perform more and more services for you as time goes by."

Did I hear someone say, "Play it again"? Apple has made that promise before—that Sherlock would gain support from other developers and offer new services. That never happened, although a guy did create a more useful Sherlock clone named Watson (www.karelia.com/watson/).

I have cried too many tears over Sherlock's failed promise. And Apple seems to agree it's a failure, as some of what Sherlock does is offered as widgets in the Mac OS X Tiger Dashboard application. Apple says third parties will develop applications for the Dashboard as well, so we'll have to wait and see.

Your Mac mini as a Media Center

Do an Internet search on "Mac mini" and "media center," and you will find a fair number of references, including some to a couple of groups planning to write open-source software to smooth the way. However, in playing with the Mac mini and experimenting, I've decided that, except for a few purposes, creating a true media center using a Mac mini is still too much of a science fair project for my liking: too much trouble, too little reward. The Mac mini does have a role, though, if you limit yourself to things that are easy to do and actually useful. I will focus on two of these: using the Mac mini as a music hub and viewing and recording programs on your television.

Using your Mac mini as a music hub

Thanks to iTunes and AirPort Express, your Mac mini is a great central repository for your music and is capable of wirelessly streaming it to speakers and stereo systems around your home. AirPort Express can output either conventional analog or digital (optical) audio, selected by plugging in the proper cable. For many people, this feature alone is worth the cost of the Mac mini (and is described in Chapter 5).

Receiving radio programs on your Mac mini

Griffin Technology (www.griffintechnology.com) offers some truly wonderful Mac accessories, many related to audio or the iPod. You should visit the Griffin Web site to see what the company offers.

Among the items you will find is the Radio Shark, an AM/FM radio receiver that attaches to a Mac (or PC) and lets you listen to over-the-air radio or record it for later listening. You can also set up automatic recording, in effect making using Radio Shark as a radio TiVo for your Mac mini.

In Chapter 10, I discuss some interesting audio applications from Rouge Amoeba Software, including Audio Hijack, which allows you to record any audio your Mac mini can play (such as from RealPlayer) and to schedule recordings of programs on the Internet. Another, Airfoil, allows you to wirelessly transmit any audio your Mac mini can play to an AirPort Express device connected to remote speakers or a stereo system.

Television and your Mac mini

If you want to use your Mac mini to record television programs, you will make the acquaintance of a German company named Elgato Systems (www.elgato.com). Elgato specializes in turning all-in-one units, like the iMac, into expensive television sets.

But the Elgato hardware and software can also be used with the Mac mini, as part of your home entertainment center, ideally also connected to your stereo system and a huge screen with a DVI input. The device you need is Elgato's EyeTV 200, discussed next.

tip   **Elgato makes an HDTV tuner for Macintosh use. However, the company does not recommend it for Macs with less than the high-end G5 processor, which leaves out the Mac mini.**

EyeTV 200

Elgato's EyeTV 200 can turn your Mac mini into a TiVo-like device, capable of recording (and displaying) television programs as you desire, up to the capacity of your hard drive. You can also use it to display live television programs on your Mac mini. I have been using EyeTV 200 with my Mac mini for a couple of months now, and they work together quite well.

The $299 EyeTV 200 can pick up broadcasts received over the air. Connect a TV antenna to the ANT IN port on the device. Likewise, you can connect a cable television feed to the ANT IN port and receive unscrambled, unencrypted channels. The benefit of receiving programming over the air or via cable is that the EyeTV's internal tuner can be controlled by the software, allowing the device to change channels as needed to record your favorite programs.

You can connect EyeTV 200 to a cable TV box or satellite receiver in either of two ways:

- If your box has audio and video outputs, connect the red and white audio jacks and the yellow video jack to the same-colored ports on the EyeTV receiver. Special three-conductor cables are available for this purpose, and you probably already have a bunch of them. This is called composite video.

  For better quality, if your cable box or satellite receiver has an S-Video output, connect it, instead of the yellow video cable, to the EyeTV. You will still need the red and white audio cables connected.

- If your cable box/satellite receiver has an RF output, connect a coaxial cable from the RF output on the box to the ANT IN port on the EyeTV 200 device. You will then tune the received signal on channel 3 or 4 on the EyeTV 200. This is not the preferred way to get a signal into EyeTV as RF is of distinctly lower quality than either the composite video or S-Video used in the first method.

The problem with either of these methods is that you have to select channels using the cable box or satellite receiver rather than the EyeTV software. That means if you want to record a program on channel 6 at 7 P.M. and another on channel 9 and 10 P.M., sometime after the end of the first program and the beginning of the second you will have to change the channel on your box. This is how some of the very first VCRs worked, and, frankly, it's stupid. But until the consumer electronics and cable/satellite industries get their acts together, it's how things are.

EyeTV 200 can also be connected to many other video devices, such as DVD players, VCRs, TiVos, and cameras. By feeding their outputs into an EyeTV connected to a Mac mini, you can record programs and edit them if you like before copying them to a CD or DVD.

You connect these devices to the composite video and S-Video inputs on the EyeTV 200 box just as you would to a cable box or satellite receiver. Sadly, the EyeTV 200 box does not have a digital input that would allow higher-quality dubs from digital sources.

To connect the EyeTV 200 box to your Mac mini, use the included FireWire cable. It's only 3 feet long, but you can buy a longer cable if necessary. There are two FireWire connections on the EyeTV 200 box. Do not try to daisy chain other FireWire-powered devices with EyeTV 200.

You have now completed the hard part of installing EyeTV 200. Installing the software is simply a matter of inserting the CD and dragging the program to your Mac mini's hard drive. The installation process includes determining what channels are available in your area, either over the air or cable, as well as establishing a TitanTV.com account for access to the online program guide.

You don't have to always be connected to the Internet to use TitanTV, which is an independent service used with a variety of PC and Mac TV tuners. The software will automatically download program information (if you tell it to) for use when you aren't online. You can also set the EyeTV software manually to record a particular channel at a specific time, but that's not as easy or as fun as pointing and clicking in the TitanTV program grid.

Getting It All Connected

It used to be easy to get video from a VCR into a TV set. The VCR contained a modulator that generated a TV signal, usually on channel 3 or 4. A piece of coaxial cable with an F screw connector on each end connected the output of the VCR and the antenna jack on the TV.

For you to view the picture from the VCR, the TV had to be tuned to the channel used by the modulator: channel 3 or 4. The picture this method produced looked like television, which was all we really had to compare it to. Cable boxes and other devices also connected to TV sets in this manner.

You can still use the ANT, cable, and RF inputs and outputs to send video and audio around your home entertainment system. But modern AV components, including the Mac mini, offer much better alternatives. I will explain what these are and how most can be used with a Mac mini.

- **Composite video.** Are you familiar with the yellow, red, and white three-wire cable assemblies used to connect AV equipment? Sure you are, because this is the most common means of making those connections. Composite video is better than RF, but you have much better alternatives. The yellow cable carries the video, and the red and white cables are used for stereo audio.

(continues on next page)

Getting It All Connected *(continued)*

- **S-Video.** This is what used to define high-end home video for most people. S-Video separates the video signal into separate color and luminance channels. With S-Video, you get a picture that starts doing justice to your DVD, satellite system, or digital camcorder. S-Video uses a round multipin connector, which is usually black. S-Video requires a separate audio connection.

- **Component video.** You might think that the three connectors—red, green, and blue—transmit those colors from your device to your screen. That's what I always assumed, but then I learned that component video separates the signal into two color components and one luminance component. That means it's a shade, so to speak, better than S-Video and finds its way into HD satellite receivers, DVD players, and cable boxes. Component video requires a separate audio connection.

- **DVI.** This is the connector that you will find on the back of your Mac mini and other Apple computers. DVI allows a digital-to-digital connection between your Mac and a screen or other video device. DVI is great for DVD players, satellite receivers, cable boxes, digital camcorders, and other devices. It also allows content providers to, in some cases, control what you can do with their content. DVI requires a separate audio connection.

  Included with your Mac mini is a DVI-to-VGA converter used to connect your Mac to a monitor that lacks a DVI input. (I recommend leaving the adapter always connected or taped to the back of the monitor so it will be available when you need it.)

  Apple also sells a $19 DVI-to-video adapter that allows your Mac mini to connect to any S-video or composite video–enabled device.

- **HDMI.** This is a digital connection that carries video and audio on a single cable. The Mac mini does not support HDMI.

- **VGA.** This is the standard PC video connection. If you want to connect a Windows PC to your new monitor, make sure it has a VGA input.

When purchasing a large home theater–style display, you need to make sure it has the appropriate connectors. Many still lack DVI, which is something you want. Also, many HDMI-equipped monitors lack a DVI connector, though some have both.

Climb in back of your TV set if you have to so you can make sure it has the inputs you need.

Accessing content remotely

The design of the Mac mini makes it easy to bring the computer into the den or family room and connect it directly to your home entertainment system. But suppose you want to keep the Mac mini on your desk and access your media content (music, photos, video, and so on) remotely?

The easiest way to do this is with a wireless AirPort network, capable of connecting all the computers (and other wireless devices as I am about to explain) in your home in a single network.

For the purpose of this chapter, I am assuming that you already have an AirPort Extreme or other 802.11g wireless network established. If you don't, that's okay, too—just return to Chapter 5 to see how to set up a home network.

But before I continue, let me offer a bit of advice: Networking Macs really is easier—not surprisingly—if you use Mac hardware. That solves any potential compatibility problems before they start and also gives you the benefit of Apple's commitment to ease of use. Creating a wireless network isn't that difficult, but if you've never done it before, the Apple tools make it pretty easy to accomplish. And yes, your Windows computers will connect to an Apple base station just fine.

And in case you're wondering, I am using an AirPort Extreme Base Station as the center of a fairly complex all-wireless network involving a DSL Internet connection, a Windows 2003 Server, a Mac mini, three Mac notebooks, an iMac, three Windows desktop systems, and a couple of Windows notebooks. I am also running three AirPort Express devices to extend the network and play iTunes in different rooms of the house. My plan is to add more AirPort Express units in the future.

AirPort Express

Apple describes AirPort Express (with iTunes) as a tool to "enjoy your iTunes music library in virtually every room of your house." The device, a small white box that plugs into a wall outlet, allows you to share a broadband connection and a USB printer and even create an "instant wireless network" when you are traveling.

Here's how I use it: After you install AirPort Express, the name of the device—one of mine is called Bedroom—appears in your iTunes player. You can then choose to have your Mac (or Windows PC) send the music from iTunes to the selected AirPort Express unit instead of to the speakers sitting next to the computer. You cannot, by the way, have both the speakers and AirPort Express playing at the same time, and a computer can send music to only one AirPort Express unit at a time, although different computers can simultaneously talk to different AirPort Express units.

Each AirPort Express unit has three ports: one for Ethernet, one for a USB printer, and one for either a standard stereo cable or an optical audio cable. Upstairs in my bedroom, the audio output of the AirPort Express unit is connected to the AUX input on a Bose Wave Radio, but it would work equally well feeding a pair of powered speakers or a stereo system.

Thanks to AirPort Express, an iTunes playlist selected on the Mac mini downstairs can play to the Bose Wave Radio at my bedside upstairs. If you think of the iTunes playlist as a commercial-free radio station that you control, you've got the idea. If you think of it as an iTunes playlist, you'll want to actually control it—skip songs, read song titles, and so on—things AirPort Express doesn't do.

For that, you will need the Keyspan Express Remote, a 17-button infrared remote-control device that connects to the USB port on the AirPort Express device, giving you the ability to control iTunes wirelessly. You can skip a song, go back a song, pause, control the volume, and issue other commands just by pointing the remote at the IR sensor in the AirPort Express unit.

The Keyspan Express Remote can do the same connected to the USB port on your Mac mini and can control other applications as well, including PowerPoint and QuickTime and Real media players. And it also works with Windows computers and applications. Not bad for $59.95.

If you want more control of your music, you'll have to either use an iPod, which has a screen and allows you to select different playlists, or place a Mac mini or other computer beside your bed.

Here's a creative use for an AirPort Express base station: Take it along with your Mac mini or another Mac or Windows portable to a party or other event. When you arrive, hook up AirPort Express to the stereo or sound system, and you can use iTunes to stream music from your computer. In Chapter 10, check out the review of MegaSeg DJ software.

What "Media Center" Means: Apple vs. Microsoft

Microsoft has a product called Windows XP Media Center Edition, and a number of companies offer PCs designed to take advantage of it. None of these have sold very well, but Microsoft has put a lot of work into this and can be expected to stick with it until it either catches on or something else replaces it as a way to bring Windows PCs into home entertainment centers.

What the Microsoft Media Center is about is media *consumption*. It allows you to watch content that is stored on your PC on a screen that is connected to the PC or to one of several devices similar to the Elgato EyeHome Digital Media Player that's sold to Mac users. These can be connected to screens in other parts of your home.

Windows Media Center also allows you to play stored music, look at your digital photos, and do the other kinds of things you'd do if you were sitting in front of your computer. Especially nice is a 10-foot user interface designed for use from across the room (for instance, when you're sitting on the couch watching TV) with a remote control. This is something I'd expect Apple to include with Mac OS at some point in the future.

As I said, Windows Media Center is about consumption. While Microsoft has some nice tools for creating digital media, they are limited and/or cost extra.

Apple, by comparison, is about media *creation*. That's why iLife is included with so many Macs, including the Mac mini. With iLife, you can edit your home videos and then burn them onto a DVD, use iTunes to create and manage a music library, and use iPhoto to edit digital photos and manage your picture collection. Apple relies (for now) on third parties for the sort of television and radio features that come with Windows Media Center PCs, but then surges ahead with the wildly popular iPod family of music playback and photo-viewing devices.

There's really nothing wrong with either approach. Both simply reflect the heritage of the companies responsible. Apple has always been strong with the people who create content, while Microsoft has always been very mass-market oriented. It's just now that the mass market has started arriving at the place Apple has been for many years.

EyeHome Digital Media Player

AirPort Express is great for sending audio around your house, but there is more to life than sound. For those other things, you need the Elgato Systems EyeHome Digital Media Player, a $219 companion product to the EyeTV tuner and personal video recording system.

EyeHome Digital Media Player allows you to access the content stored on your Mac mini, such as music, video, movies, and photos, from your TV and home entertainment system. EyeHome includes its own IR remote control, which you can use to control media playback using a user interface that appears on your monitor.

The media player connects to your monitor using S-Video, component video, or composite video signals for video, and RCA or S/PDIF digital connections for sound. The media player is intended for use away from your computer, so it requires a connection to your home network: via Ethernet or AirPort Express.

Using the media player with video requires the higher speed offered by an AirPort Extreme Base Station. The older, original AirPort is adequate only for music and pictures. The media player does not support HDTV video.

You can use the EyeHome player to watch movies stored on your computer in a variety of formats, including those used by the EyeTV system. You cannot, however, watch a DVD from your Mac mini's DVD drive. Only content on your hard drive can be played on the EyeHome player, and, besides, most DVD content is encrypted.

Another gotcha is that your iMovie files will have to be converted to a supported format before EyeHome can play them. QuickTime movies are not supported. Some iTunes music (MP3, WAV, and AIFF formats) will play through the device. Encrypted AAC files, such as your Apple Music Store purchases, will not.

Even with these significant limitations, EyeHome is a good way to extend digital content stored on your Mac mini to other rooms in your house.

10

Recommended Software

The world of Mac software, of course, extends far beyond the applications included on your Mac mini. If you can do it on a computer, chances are good there's software available to do it on a Mac mini.

As you read this chapter, you will learn:

- About some useful programs for your Mac mini.

- Where to get more information and downloads for the applications described.

In this chapter, you will find single-page descriptions, in alphabetical order, of some of the software a group of friends and I use everyday and recommend to others. These are not actual reviews—just pointers to some useful applications. No attempt has been made to make this a comprehensive list. You will also find software described in other parts of this book, especially Chapter 9.

In addition, Appendix B lists a number of Mac mini resources, many of which include software reviews. Especially be sure to visit *Macworld* magazine (www.macworld.com) and VersionTracker (www.versiontracker.com).

Most of the software products in this book are available on a trial basis as downloads. If you have a broadband connection (or access to one), this is a great way to try out a program before having to pay for it. Even Microsoft Office is available on a trial basis. You can find all the URLs for this chapter and the entire book at www.peachpit.com/coursey.

Airfoil

What: Allows any application to feed speakers attached to an AirPort Express Base Station

By: Rogue Amoeba Software

Cost: $25

Download: www.rogueamoeba.com

Apple equipped iTunes to transmit music from its own library to remote speakers attached to AirPort Express Base Stations. It can also transmit radio stations from its own quite limited directory of Internet stations.

That leaves a tremendous amount of audio that iTunes cannot transmit to AirPort Express. And for that orphan audio, we have Airfoil, a utility that allows any audio from your Mac mini to be transmitted to remote speakers attached to an AirPort Express Base Station. Airfoil allows you to select the application whose audio you want to transmit as well as the AirPort Express you want to transmit the audio to.

The figure shows Airfoil sending RealPlayer audio to an AirPort Express device.

Why I like it: For anyone whose listening interests run beyond iTunes, this is an essential utility. I use it to transmit Internet radio, such as the BBC and XM Radio online, to speakers in my bedroom and the home theater system.

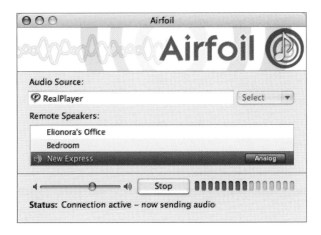

AuctionSieve

What: eBay auction filtering utility

By: Hashbang Pty. Ltd.

Cost: Freeware

Download: www.auctionsieve.com

AuctionSieve is a free utility that automates searches of auction listings on eBay. It saves you from having to check individual searches on the auction site, letting you run multiple custom queries simultaneously. It then presents the results in a single pane, with the best matches at the top.

The software can be set up by browsing eBay categories, entering the category ID, or specifying search words. Adding Catch Words to a search causes all listings with the words to be grouped together. Specifying Trash Words prevents AuctionSieve from picking up listings that contain those terms. You can also filter by number of bids, price, or Buy It Now Price and include or exclude specific currencies and categories. You can add listings to your Watchlist and then save more time by turning on the Ignore Auctions Already Seen filter.

The figure shows the main interface after AuctionSieve executed multiple searches for airline china and memorabilia.

Why I like it: AuctionSieve can help eBay addicts find better bargains in less time.

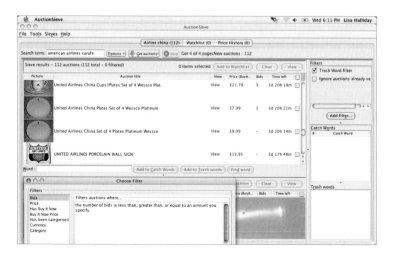

Audio Hijack Pro

What: Software that allows you to record anything your Mac mini can hear

By: Rogue Amoeba Software

Cost: $32

Download: www.rogueamoeba.com

For television, I have a TiVo; for the Internet and my Mac mini, I have Audio Hijack Pro, which allows me to record and schedule the recording of anything my Mac mini can hear. It also records from iTunes, which is a plus for iPod users.

The program records to a variety of formats and includes plug-ins to improve the quality of your recordings. It's a good choice for converting vinyl or cassette music to a digital format.

The figure shows the program recording an audio stream from RealPlayer, also shown.

Why I like it: I like this utility because I can't always be sitting at the computer when an interesting program is on. But it has plenty of other uses as well.

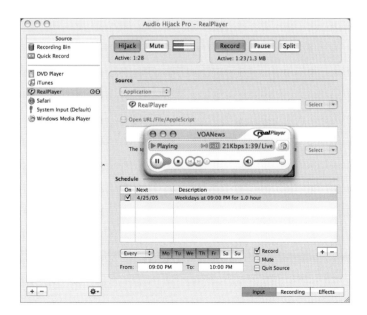

Business Card Composer

What: Business card designer

By: BeLight Software, Ltd.

Cost: $39.95 + shipping, boxed version; $34.95 downloaded version

Download: www.belightsoft.com

Business Card Composer's sole function is to help you design professional-looking business cards. It comes with a wide variety of pre-designed templates and categories of clip art and photos. It can also access images in your iPhoto albums via a menu option.

You begin the process by choosing the orientation and the card stock on which you're planning to print from a long list of popular vendors' products. Then you can choose a modifiable template or a blank card. Fields on the card will automatically import information from Mac OS X's Address Book entries. And if you want to have your cards printed professionally, a link lets you send the job to an online printing company.

The figure shows a card created using one of the templates, plus the Properties, Colors, and Fonts palettes and the Food clip art collection.

Why I like it: Business Card Composer makes it easy to create business cards you'll be proud to pull out of your pocket.

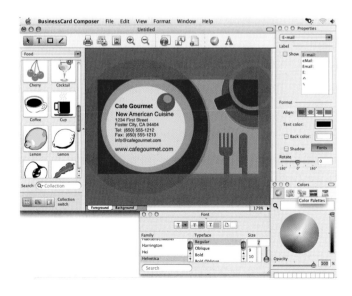

Canvas

What: Illustration, photo editing, page layout, and presentation software

By: ACD Systems of America

Cost: $349.95 regular version; $549.99 scientific imaging version; $649.99 GIS version

Download: www.acdamerica.com

Canvas is a powerful, precision illustration package that also includes photo retouching, page layout, and presentation capabilities. It competes with some of Adobe's Creative Suite tools and is available for both Mac and Windows. Its interface is cleaner than most drawing and page layout programs because it defaults to opening only one floating palette. Other palettes and dialog boxes are easily accessible via a tabbed tool-bar. Novices can quickly familiarize themselves with tool functionality by using Dynamic Help. Other nice features include the ability to break large graphics into pieces to facilitate faster Web downloads, and sprites, which can be used to apply transparency effects to any object.

The figure shows two documents: a page layout and an illustration. In the center is the main drawing palette.

Why I like it: Canvas packs much of the functionality of several high-end software packages into one moderately priced application. It offers great value for the money.

Corel Painter

What: Painting and illustration software

By: Corel Corporation

Cost: $399 download; $429 box

Download: www.corel.com

Corel Painter helps you create digital paintings that look like they've been made using real-world media. More than 30 customizable brushes simulate the look of artists' oils, watercolor, acrylics, pastels, crayons, and more. Painter allows you to control the texture of the painting surface, and brushes interact with the grain, just as they would in real life. You can also mix custom colors on a palette, just as an artist can do with real paint.

Painter offers a host of animation features and supports scripting to automate repetitive operations. It can import from and export to most popular file formats, including PSD, TIFF, BMP, TARGA, JPEG, PICT, AI, MOV, and AVI.

The figure shows a painting that painter and Peachpit author Cher Threinen-Pendarvis created in Painter, along with the Artists' Oils control, Mixer palette, and Color Sets window.

Why I like it: With Corel Painter, you can explore your inner Van Gogh right on your Mac mini.

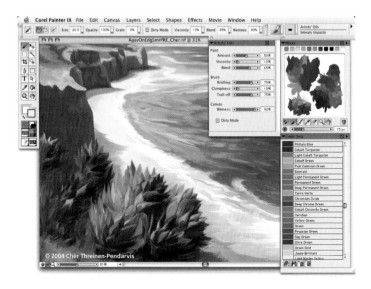

DayLite

What: Customer relationship management software

By: Marketcircle, Inc.

Cost: $149

Download: www.marketcircle.com

DayLite is a customer relationship management (CRM) application that helps you record and track interactions with your clients and maintain their contact information. It has a built-in calendaring program to help salespeople keep track of their schedules. It is the easiest-to-set-up CRM program I've found on any platform for multiple users sharing the same data.

Unlike many CRM solutions, DayLite also lets you keep track of specific sales possibilities by entering them as "opportunities," with potential deal values and probabilities that the deal will close. Once a deal is closed, you can create a project to help you meet delivery deadlines.

The program runs on the OpenBase database engine. It can integrate e-mail from Mac OS X Mail in the DayLite database.

The figure shows the Contact view of the sample database.

Why I like it: DayLite is a low-cost yet powerful CRM solution that can grow with small businesses.

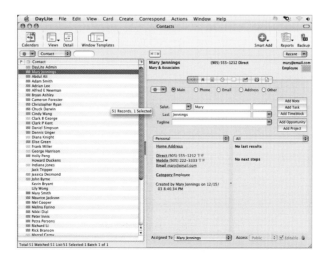

DeltaGraph

What: Charting and graphing software

By: Red Rock Software, Inc.

Cost: $299

Download: www.redrocksw.com

DeltaGraph takes charting and graphing to a level beyond what you can do with Microsoft Excel. It offers more than 60 additional chart types, as well as myriad customization options. For your charts that need to look good in print, DeltaGraph even includes support for CMYK and PANTONE colors. It also offers export options that Excel doesn't, including the ability to export to JPG, PSD, EPS, TIF, and PCT formats.

The figure shows tips for a Build-Up chart option, including pointers on how to create cleaner-looking charts.

Why I like it: DeltaGraph helps you create charts and graphs that stand out from the crowd.

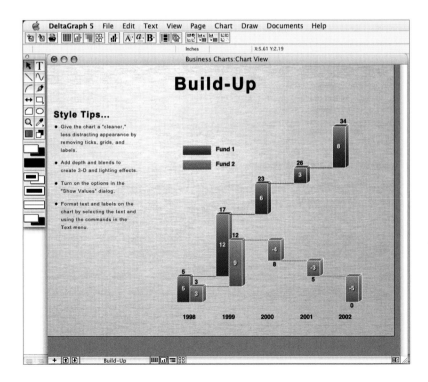

DiskWarrior

What: Disk repair utility

By: Alsoft, Inc.

Cost: $79.99

Download: www.alsoft.com

DiskWarrior can repair damaged disks and recover data feared gone for good. Instead of simply repairing damage to the disk and possibly writing over usable data, it searches the drive for all salvageable data and then rebuilds the directory structure with only the usable data to help ensure maximum data recovery.

If you install DiskWarrior before you have problems, it monitors your drive to alert you to potential failure. It can also optimize your directory for maximum performance.

The figure shows DiskWarrior's main directory rebuilding interface.

Why I like it: DiskWarrior can make recovering your data as painless as possible and sometimes even keep the loss from happening in the first place. You may never have a disk crash, but when you do, this is the product you need.

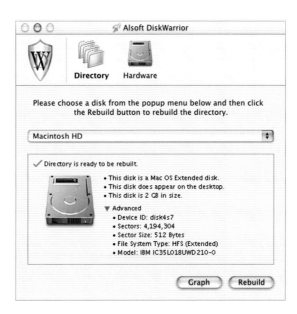

FastTrack Schedule

What: Project scheduling software

By: AEC Software

Cost: $299

Download: www.aecsoft.com

FastTrack Schedule offers powerful scheduling tools to keep your projects on track. It provides predesigned templates and modifiable examples for many industry and personal projects. It includes a very thorough tutorial to get you up and running quickly, and most scheduling elements are customizable for maximum flexibility. FastTrack's three main views—Schedule, Calendar, and Resource—also provide valuable perspectives on your projects. FastTrack lets you save schedules in many graphic formats for publishing in documents or on the Web. Your schedules can also go mobile via a $99 version of the software that's available for Palm OS.

The figure shows the Business Startup sample schedule in two views. The Schedule view is on the left, and the Resource view is on the right.

Why I like it: FastTrack Schedule makes it easy to track complicated projects and keep tabs on your progress.

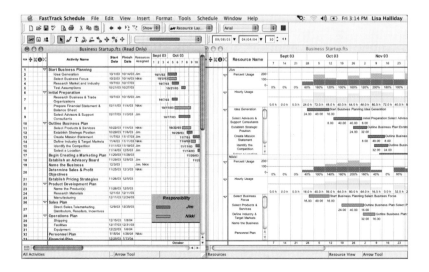

FileMaker Pro

What: Database software

By: FileMaker, Inc. (an Apple subsidiary)

Cost: $299

Download: www.filemaker.com

FileMaker Pro is a powerful but easy-to-use database that was origi-
nally designed for the Mac. It comes with 30 starter database applications that can be customized with point-and-click ease. If you need to
create your own application, a Layout and Report Assistant is there to
guide you through the process.

Most types of information can be imported into FileMaker, including
Microsoft Excel files, digital images, and even movies. FileMaker inte-
grates with Microsoft Office applications, allowing mail merges with
Microsoft Word and mass e-mailings via Microsoft Outlook or
Entourage. You can even provide occasional user access or information
via the Web using FileMaker's one-click Web publishing feature.

The figure shows three views of the application: a list view (left), a
detail view of a company (center), and a detail view of a product,
including images (right).

Why I like it: FileMaker makes it possible for small businesses to set
up databases without spending a fortune on programmers.

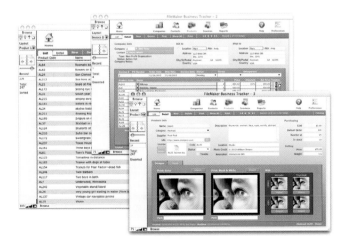

Final Draft

What: Screenwriting software

By: Final Draft, Inc.

Cost: $229

Download: www.finaldraft.com

Final Draft is a specialized word processor for writing scripts and screenplays. It automatically formats each element of the screenplay (scene heading, action, dialogue transition, and so on). You can also generate several different reports with it, such as location, scene, and character reports. It includes multiple templates for movie screenplays and stage plays, and even ones for over 50 popular television shows (some no longer in production). The latter group offers tips such as the number of acts and pages a specific show usually uses. The software also can generate "index cards" that can be rearranged, making scene reordering easy. Final Draft also allows Internet collaboration.

The figure shows the product's user interface with one of the predesigned show templates, this one for the medical drama "ER."

Why I like it: Final Draft frees you from having to worry about mundane, but important, formatting conventions. Even a novice can generate a professional-looking script with it.

Fire

What: Multi-service instant messaging client

By: epicware, Inc., and open-source developers

Cost: Freeware

Download: fire.sourceforge.net

Fire is a free instant messaging client that can access most popular IM services, including AIM, ICQ, IRC, Jabber, MSN, Yahoo Messenger, and Apple Bonjour (formerly called Rendezvous).

If you're concerned about privacy issues, Fire supports Gnu Privacy Guard (GPG) encryption on every service except Yahoo! Messenger. The software can be customized in myriad ways so users can have the look, feel, and sound effects they prefer. Fire also lets Mac users choose among 22 Macintosh voice options for speech.

The figure shows the Buddies and Accounts windows, along with the Fire Preferences dialog box and its various customization items.

Why I like it: Fire can help users of multiple instant messaging systems simplify their online social lives.

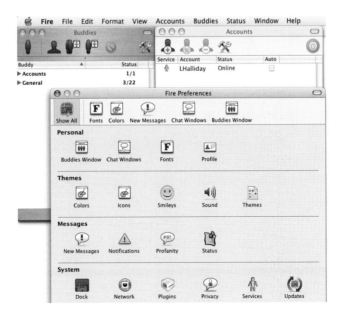

Freeway

What: Graphical Web development tool

By: Softpress Systems Ltd.

Cost: Express version: $89 download, $99 box;
Pro version: $229 download, $249 box

Download: www.softpress.com

Freeway lets users with little to no HTML coding experience create compelling Web sites. The entry-level version, Freeway Express, includes 29 predesigned templates and lets you drag and drop graphics and text onto the page. Freeway automatically compresses the graphics for the Web and generates the HTML code. When you need to upload edited pages to your server, a "smart upload" feature speeds the process by uploading only changes, rather than the entire pages.

The Pro version of Freeway adds support for Cascading Style Sheets (CSS) and layers and some advanced graphic handling capabilities, as well as the ability to automate some aspects of the design function.

The figure shows a Web site under construction in Freeway Express using one of the supplied templates.

Why I like it: Freeway makes it easier for non-Web developers to get their Web sites up and running. It is not as easy to use as Microsoft FrontPage, however.

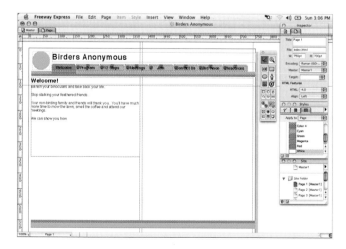

Grammarian PRO X

What: Grammar and style checker

By: Linguisoft, Inc.

Cost: $39.95

Download: www.linguisoft.com

This is the most comprehensive grammar and style correction tool that I have used, regardless of operating system. The advice it offers is highly customizable to match a variety of writing styles. Grammarian also offers readability statistics for those interested in such things. (The program tells me that this section is written at about the ninth-grade reading level.)

Grammarian can either "look over your shoulder" and point out errors as you commit them or be brought to bear during a final edit-and-polish stage of your writing project.

The figure reveals that I have a "squinting" modifier (*occasionally*) in the next paragraph.

Why I like it: Grammarian can find more errors in someone's writing than the toughest high school English teacher—which means it can keep even a careful writer from occasionally looking stupid. (So it does a lot for me—when I remember to use it.)

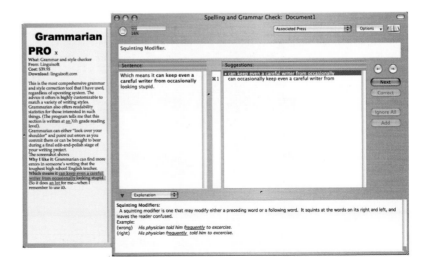

GraphicConverter

What: Graphic file conversion and photo editing software

By: Lemke Software GmbH

Cost: $30 download, $35 CD

Download: www.lemkesoft.com

GraphicConverter does exactly what the name implies: converts graphic files from one format to another. But it goes far beyond what the typical graphics program can handle. It can import more than 175 file formats, ranging from the newest (JPEG2000) to the most common (JPG, PDF, GIF) to the truly obscure (files from old computers and graphics programs and multiple microscope and medical imaging formats). If you have a graphics file with an unrecognizable extension that you need to open, this program is a good place to start. It can also export files in more than 75 formats.

In addition to its conversion prowess, GraphicConverter offers more sophisticated photo editing tools than you would expect at this price, including gamma correction and color permutation.

The figure shows some of the file formats that GraphicConverter can save to.

Why I like it: GraphicConverter is an affordable "Swiss Army Knife" program that's useful to have around.

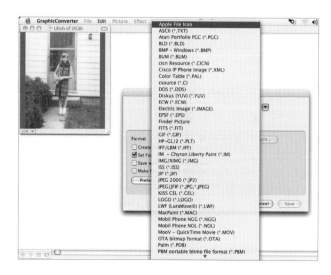

iPulse

What: System monitoring utility that provides an under-the-hood look at what your Mac is doing

By: iconfactory

Cost: $12.95

Download: www.iconfactory.com

Most people will never care what the temperature of their CPU is, how memory is being used, or the precise bandwidth of their network connection. For those who do, there's iPulse.

Roll your cursor over iPulse, and the program displays a pop-up window. By moving the cursor, you can inspect system-level data, including memory, disk usage, CPU usage, system load, motherboard temperature, and network activity. Get all the information you need from the info window or just watch iPulse's gauges on your desktop.

Understanding those gauges, however, is nonintuitive. The gauge shown in the figure displays 20 parameters. If you can remember what each one is, you are doing much better than I've been able to. I just rely on the pop-up windows when I want to know something.

Why I like it: There are many system monitoring programs available for the Mac mini. This one provides all the relevant information and does it with style to spare.

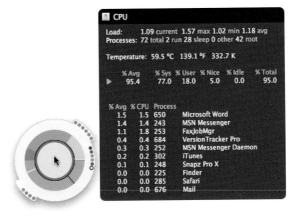

iStumbler

What: Utility for finding wireless networks

By: Alf Watt

Cost: $1 donation requested

Download: www.istumbler.com

iStumbler is a free, open-source tool for finding AirPort or other 802.11 wireless networks, Bluetooth devices, and mDNS services used by Bonjour. It also provides GPS locations if you have a GPS device connected to your Mac mini.

While most useful to laptop users, who can use iStumbler to find Wi-Fi hot spots, Mac mini users can use the software to find the best place to locate their computer or wireless base station for highest signal strength. It can also be used to avoid interference from other base stations nearby.

The figure displays iStumbler's main window, showing my wireless network.

Why I like it: iStumbler is easy to use and provides a wealth of information about the networks your Mac mini can "see." Use the displayed signal strength to locate your Mac mini and AirPort base station.

Mactracker

What: Macintosh history database

By: Ian Page

Cost: Freeware (contributions accepted)

Download: www.mactracker.ca

Mactracker is a desktop database application that provides detailed technical information on every Macintosh model ever made (including the short-lived Mac OS clones), as well as information on Apple printers and peripheral devices, cameras, Newtons, iPods, and versions of Mac OS X.

In addition to the technical information, most entries include a small picture and short history of each computer or device. Macintosh entries even have buttons that will play that model's startup and death chimes.

The figure shows Mactracker's category lists, along with two entries from the database: a technical overview of the Macintosh Color Classic and a history of the Apple Lisa/Macintosh mouse.

Why I like it: If you're curious to see how the Macintosh has evolved over the years, Mactracker is a good place to start.

MegaSeg

What: DJ software

By: Fidelity Media, Inc.

Cost: $199

Download: www.megaseg.com

MegaSeg lets you live your dream of becoming a DJ. You can easily categorize, select, and order the songs you want to play, create a playlist, and get the party hopping. It can import any sound file that QuickTime supports, including MP3 and WAV files, and can scan your iTunes library or connected iPod for new music. It can segue between tracks with a customizable crossfade.

The manual is filled with helpful professional hints, such as how to set up a sound system and to how keep music sounding fresh by not playing more than two tracks in a row by any male or female vocalist.

The figure shows the product interface with a playlist on the right and the music library on the left. Note the controls for DJ functions.

Why I like it: Whether you want to run your own little radio station, play music for others at a party, or simply entertain yourself while you work, MegaSeg helps your create perfect playlists and ends dead air for good.

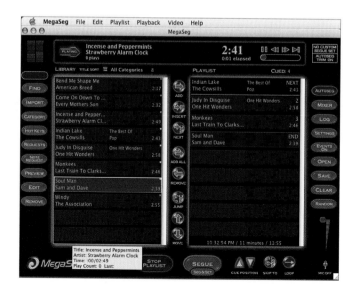

MYOB AccountEdge

What: Software suite for small-business management

By: MYOB US, Inc.

Cost: $299

Download: www.myob.com

MYOB AccountEdge offers small businesses an easy way to manage their accounting, banking, sales, payroll, inventory, and contacts all in a single application.

The simple, intuitive interface makes setup and data entry straight-forward. AccountEdge's automatic reports and analyses also help you easily keep tabs on how your business is doing and detect problem areas. MYOB also offers a number of services for small businesses, which are integrated with the AccountEdge software. These include payroll, employee check direct deposit, credit card merchant services, and vendor payment.

The figure shows AccountEdge's main Command Center screen, which offers access to all of the program's modules.

Why I like it: MYOB AccountEdge is an economical small-business management solution you don't have to spend hours learning to use.

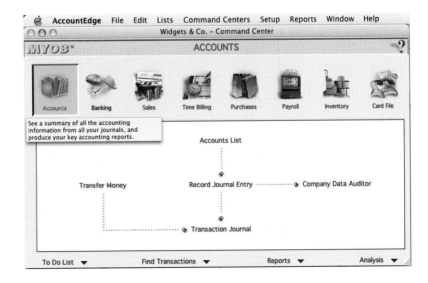

NetNewsWire

What: RSS newsreader—and more

By: Ranchero Software

Cost: Single-user license, $24.95; multiuser licenses, $19.95 per person; Lite version, freeware

Download: www.ranchero.com

Clifford Colby, my long-suffering editor at Peachpit Press, says NetNewsWire is "the first software in years that changed how I work." Cliff subscribes to 30 or so RSS news feeds, from the Washington *Post* and eWeek to a friend's San Francisco Giants baseball blog. This application lets him check all the headlines in a couple of minutes and then read the pieces that interest him.

"There was no way I would accomplish much else if I checked 30-something Web sites throughout the day and didn't have a newsreader. I know Safari can show RSS feeds now, but I like how NetNewsWire displays and handles feeds."

The figure shows the news feeds Cliff follows, as displayed and managed by NetNewsWire.

Why I Like It: Like Cliff, I think news feeds deserve their own application (or should appear in a mail client). This is a very nice client.

Nicecast

What: Internet broadcasting utility

By: Rogue Amoeba Software

Cost: $40

Download: www.rogueamoeba.com

Nicecast turns your Mac mini into an Internet radio station. This is not something for everyone, but it could be more useful than it at first might seem. For example, a friend of mine uses Nicecast to Webcast his iTunes music library so he can listen to it in his office or send music to parties. Another friend has Nicecast connected to a radio scanner so that members of his radio club can listen to fire calls. You can also use it to feed a larger radio server at a site such as Live365.com.

The figure shows three Nicecast windows for controlling the Webcast, server selection, and special effects. Note that you can use external servers—such as Shoutcast and Live365—if you don't have enough bandwidth on your Internet connection to support the number of listeners you desire.

Why I like it: Because I'm a radio geek. I even have call letters: N5FDL.

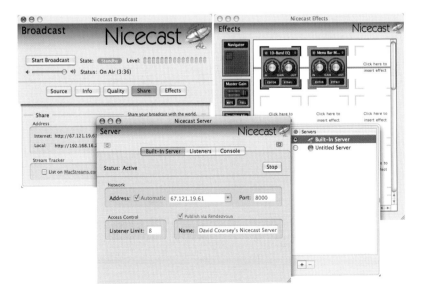

NoteBook

What: Outlining and idea organizing software

By: Circus Ponies Software

Cost: $49.95; $29.95 academic license

Download: www.circusponies.com

NoteBook lets you create tabbed digital notebooks to organize thoughts and information and to manage simple projects. With a friendly interface resembling a spiral-bound paper notebook, NoteBook lets you categorize contents with keywords and separate sections with tabs. You can also add files, voice annotations, video clips, or images, or clip information from any Mac OS X application via a Services menu.

To use NoteBook as a project manager, you can assign action-item status to entries by adding check boxes, due dates, and priorities. The software automatically creates several indices for each notebook, including ones for text, Internet addresses, to-do items, and due dates.

Notebooks can be exported to HTML text, RTF, RTFD, and OPML formats if you want to share them with someone who doesn't have the NoteBook software.

The figure shows a sample page from a cookbook created in NoteBook.

Why I like it: NoteBook makes it easy and fun to organize information and create projects. It's a great product.

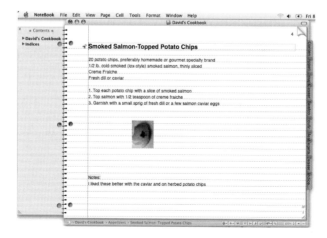

OmniGraffle

What: Software for creating charts and diagrams

By: Omni Development, Inc.

Cost: $69.95; $119.95 for Pro version

Download: www.omnigroup.com

Windows users moving to the Macintosh sometimes ask about whether Microsoft Visio, the charting and diagramming product, is available for Mac. It isn't. OmniGraffle is the program that replaces Visio for Mac users. It reads and writes Visio files.

For those who don't use Visio, OmniGraffle offers an easy way to create good-looking versions of the sorts of things we draw on napkins, place-mats, and legal pads. Think of it as a program for making your ideas presentable. It is useful for more than creating diagrams—for instance, for adding callouts to photographs.

The figure shows the making of a diagram in OmniGraffle and some of the tools available.

Why I like it: The program is easy to use and always gives me great results—an excellent product.

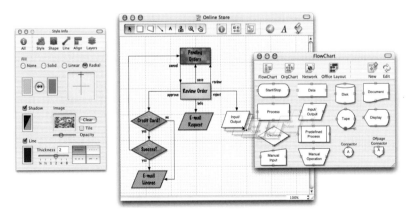

OmniOutliner

What: Outlining software

By: Omni Development, Inc.

Cost: $39.95; $69.95 for Pro version

Download: www.omnigroup.com

I've always been amazed that Microsoft hasn't built a better outliner into Office. The outline view in Word doesn't allow you to create much of an outline. So for the task of keeping my ideas organized, I use OmniOutliner. There's not much to say about the program besides that it does what it promises and does it with the flair you'd expect on a Macintosh.

The figure shows a very nontraditional outline. Yes, OmniOutliner can produce plain outlines, too. Have it your way.

Why I like it: OmniOutliner helps you create outlines ranging from utilitarian to the extreme—a very nice program. (The program competes in some ways with NoteBook, from Circus Ponies, described earlier in this chapter.)

Pagesender

What: Fax software

By: SmileOnMyMac, LLC

Cost: $29.99

Download: www.smileonmymac.com

Pagesender lets you fax or e-mail anything you can print. It also receives faxes using your fax modem, eFax, jConnect, EasyLink, or MaxEmail. You can drag and drop recipient names from most popular address books, including Address Book, Microsoft Entourage, and Outlook Express. The program works with most popular e-mail programs, including Outlook Express, Entourage, Eudora, and even Claris Emailer. Nice features include the ability to attach PDF documents to faxes, pause and resume while sending faxes, and automate fax and e-mail blasts using AppleScript.

The figure shows the Out folder and the Modem Preferences dialog box.

Why I like it: Pagesender makes it as easy as possible to send and receive faxes via your computer. (This application is a favorite of Mac tech guru Ernie Mariette.)

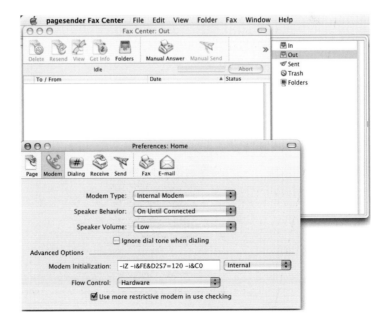

Photoshop Elements

What: Editing and organizational software for digital photography

By: Adobe Systems, Inc.

Cost: $89.99 CD ROM; $79.99 downloaded

Download: www.adobe.com

Photoshop Elements brings much of the power of Adobe's professional Photoshop program to the digital photo hobbyist. It imports photos from digital cameras, scanners, CDs, and storage media and provides a photo organizer.

The Quick Fix workspace allows quick adjustments such as red-eye corrections and cropping, while the Standard Edit workspace is where the more professional color and lighting adjustment tools and features such as layers and filters reside. When you're finished editing, Photoshop Elements helps you share photos by automatically resizing them for e-mailing and allowing you to preview them in different file formats and settings before you save them for the Web.

The figure shows the more advanced Standard Edit workspace, which contains all of the tools in the Quick Fix space and more. The File Browser, with thumbnails of stored photos, is open in the center.

Why I like it: Photoshop Elements is all the Photoshop most users will ever need at a fraction of the price of its full professional counterpart.

Remote Desktop Connection

What: Allows remote viewing of a Windows desktop

By: Microsoft Corp.

Cost: Free

Download: www.microsoft.com/mac

Microsoft RDC is a useful utility that not everyone can use. If you have a Windows XP Professional Edition machine or one of several Microsoft server flavors, RDC allows you to connect to it from your Mac mini. Once you are connected, the Windows desktop from the remote computer appears, and you can operate the computer as if you were sitting at the Windows machine's keyboard.

The figure shows the desktop of my Windows Small Business Server as viewed from RDC on my Mac mini. I can also control my Windows XP Pro desktop the same way.

Why I like it: If you already have a Windows XP Pro machine or a Windows server (I have both), RDC makes it easy to access them remotely, even over the Internet. Most often, I use RDC when I need to make changes on the server but don't want to walk downstairs. I don't recommend running applications over RDC if you can avoid it.

Retrospect

What: Backup software

By: EMC Dantz

Cost: $129 Desktop version for one stand-alone and two additional networked computers; versions also available for more computers

Download: www.dantz.com

Retrospect makes backing up your files easy. It asks if you need to back up networked or stand-alone machines, what media you want to back up to, how often you want to back up, and if you want to switch between two sets of media, in case one becomes damaged. It then creates a script to automate the backup process. You can also perform immediate, unscheduled backups. To speed the process, Retrospect doesn't perform incremental or differential backups, but backs up only entire files that are new or that have changed since the first complete backup. A repair tool lets you fix or rebuild a backup set; another tool verifies that a backup set is readable. For recovery from a really bad failure, the Retrospect CD provides a bootable solution.

The figure shows the main menu on the left and the Immediate Backup dialog box on the right.

Why I like it: Retrospect makes backing up as painless as possible. It sets the standard for backup products on the Macintosh platform and also lets you back up networked Windows machines.

Snapz Pro X

What: Screen capture software

By: Ambrosia Software, Inc.

Cost: $29; $69 with QuickTime movie feature

Download: www.ambrosiasw.com

Snapz Pro X played an important role in helping this book take shape. It's an easy-to-use utility for capturing images off a Mac mini's screen so that you can show them to someone else. All the screen shots in this book were made using Snapz Pro X.

Besides still images, Snapz Pro X can capture full-motion video of anything on your screen, complete with digital audio and an optional microphone voice-over. Think of it as a digital video camera for your screen. Snapz Pro X makes short work of creating training videos, producing product demos, creating tutorials, archiving streaming video, and capturing anything else on the screen that you can think of.

The figure shows the program's control palette.

Why I like it: If you need screen shots—or movies—this is the best way I have found to create them.

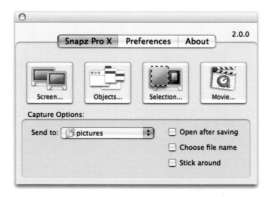

StickyBrain

What: Note manager

By: Chronos LC

Cost: $39.99

Download: www.chronosnet.com

StickyBrain uses a file box/drawer metaphor to help you organize and store notes. You can create notes in StickyBrain or import text or RTF files or Apple Stickies. StickyBrain even lets you search and view notes in other applications and e-mail notes from most popular e-mail clients. It also includes some helpful reference lists in note form, such as lists of area codes and U.S. and metric weights and measures.

The software offers good integration with .Mac via a direct button on the icon bar. It also ties in with the Mac OS X Address Book and can synch with Palm devices and iPods.

The figure shows StickyBrain's main interface with one of the product's included reference lists (Emergency Preparation Checklists) in the lower pane.

Why I like it: StickyBrain lets you turn all of your notes and information into a searchable database without the hassle of creating and querying a database.

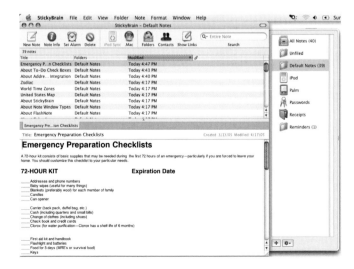

Timbuktu Pro

What: Remote computing software

By: Netopia, Inc.

Cost: $179.95 twin pack for Macintosh; $199.95 twin pack for Macintosh and Windows

Download: www.netopia.com

Timbuktu Pro allows you to control distant computers from your local machine over the Internet, over your LAN, or modem to modem. With it, you can access your files remotely, collaborate with others, or provide technical support by connecting to any other machine that also has Timbuktu Pro installed. You can view others' computer screens or let them view yours. Macintosh users can connect with and control Windows machines and vice versa using Timbuktu Pro. As long as each computer has a copy of of Timbuktu installed, no additional software is necessary.

The figure shows the New Connection and Preferences dialog boxes, along with a menu of action buttons, on the left.

Why I like it: With Timbuktu Pro, you're never too far away to access another computer.

Toast with Jam

What: Disk burning and music mixing and mastering suite

By: Roxio, Inc.

Cost: $199.95

More Information: www.roxio.com

Toast with Jam helps you master and burn CDs and DVDs that include bells and whistles sure to amaze your friends. Picking up where Apple iLife leaves off, this application bundle lets you create DVDs with Hollywood-style Dolby Digital sound, create professional-quality CD redbook specification masters, and much more.

You can produce Video CDs, Super Video CDs, and DVDs with menus, navigation buttons, and chapters (chapters are available only on DVD; music DVDs can be 36 hours long). CD Spin Doctor 2, an included application, lets you digitize your vinyl records and tapes or record live audio performances.

Toast with Jam also helps you turn still photos into movies complete with soundtracks and pan and zoom effects. The figure shows ToastAnywhere, a feature that lets you share CD or DVD recorders with other Toast users over a network and even over the Internet.

Why I like it: Toast with Jam can help bring out your inner movie or music producer.

VueScan

What: Scanning and OCR software

By: Hamrick Software

Cost: $49.99 standard edition; $89.85 professional edition

Download: www.hamrick.com

VueScan is advanced scanning software that can help your scanner work better. It supports more than 400 scanners and 157 camera raw files. The program excels at transparency scanning—supporting more than 100 brands of negative film—and at scanning faded slides and prints. It can also handle batch scanning.

The software automatically adjusts image color balance, saving you from having to do this later in a photo editor. Scans can be saved as PDF files and even as TIFF and JPEG files simultaneously at different resolutions. VueScan also includes optical character recognition that is integrated with the scanning software.

The figure shows the default Start screen.

Why I like it: VueScan can help you get more out of your scanner with less work, and the inclusion of OCR functionality means you won't have to buy a separate OCR program.

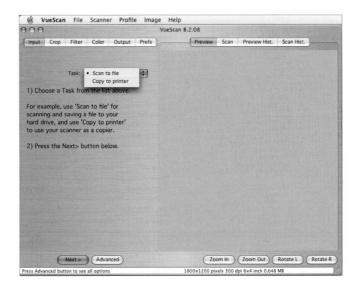

A

Keyboard
Shortcuts

If you've been using a Windows computer, probably the first thing you'll notice after you set up your Mac mini is that you don't have a two-button mouse. (If you really miss your two-button mouse, you can buy one from a handful of third-party companies that make them for the Mac.) You can still get to an item's shortcut menu—called a *contextual menu* on the Mac—however, through a keyboard shortcut: Hold down the Control key while clicking an item, and a contextual menu pops up.

The second thing you may notice is that your Mac's keyboard doesn't have a Ctrl key. Instead, you see a key with a cloverleaf-like symbol and the Apple logo. Apple calls this the Command key, and it behaves like Windows' Ctrl key. You'll also find an Option key, which performs functions similar to Windows' Alt key, and a Control key, which helps compensate for the lack of a second button on your mouse.

But like Windows, Mac OS X offers numerous useful keyboard shortcuts. After you get used to the one-button mouse and new keys, these
shortcuts can save you a lot of time. The list in this appendix isn't
comprehensive (by working your way through the various menus,
you can find many of the shortcuts).

General Shortcuts

To do this action	Use this shortcut
Move highlighted item to Trash	Command-Delete
Empty Trash	Command-Shift-Delete
Empty Trash with no warning dialog	Option-Empty Trash
Create a new Finder window	Command-N
Create a new folder	Command-Shift-N
Go to your Home directory	Command-Shift-H
Go to your Applications folder	Command-Shift-A
Duplicate an item	Command-D
Create an alias	Command-L
Add to Favorites	Command-T
Find	Command-F
Get help	Command-?
Log out	Command-Shift-Q
Turn off your computer	Power button

Menu Shortcuts

To do this action	Use this shortcut
Undo	Command-Z
Cut	Command-X
Copy	Command-C
Paste	Command-V
View as icons	Command-1
View as List	Command-2
View as Columns	Command-3

Window Shortcuts

To do this action	Use this shortcut
Close a window	Command-W
Close all open windows	Option-click Close button
Minimize a window	Command-M
Minimize all open windows	Option-click Minimize button
Hide all application windows except the one you're in	Command-Option-H
Move a window without making it active	Command-drag window
Choose a folder that contains the current folder	Command-click window title

Dock and Other Shortcuts

To do this action	Use this shortcut
Hide or show the Dock	Command-Option-D
Change the size of the Dock	Drag the dividing line
See a Dock item's contextual menu	Control-click an icon in the Dock
Quit an open application	Click a running application's icon and choose Quit
Force-quit an application	Option-click a running application's icon and choose Force Quit
Switch from one open application to the next	Command-Tab
To reverse the order of switching between applications	Command-Shift-Tab
Hide the active application	Command-H
Quit the selected application	Command-Q
Force an application to open when you drag a document into it	Command-Option

Dialog Shortcuts

To do this action	Use this shortcut
Select the next area of the dialog	Tab
Select default	Return or Enter
Cancel	Esc
Close the dialog	Esc-period (.) or Command-period (.)
Select folders above or below the current item (Save and Open dialogs)	Up and down arrows
Scroll list up	Page Up
Scroll list down	Page Down

Icon Shortcuts

To do this action	Use this shortcut
Select an icon by the first letter of its name	Letter key
Select the next icon	Arrow keys
Select the next icon alphabetically	Tab
Add an icon to the selection	Command-click
Select adjacent icons in a list	Shift-click
Select or deselect nonadjacent icons in a list	Command-click
Select all icons	Command-A
Highlight the name of a selected icon	Return
Display the contextual menu	Control-click the icon

Startup Shortcuts

To do this action	Use this shortcut
Start from a CD	C
Select a startup disk (on some computers)	Option
Prevent startup items from opening	Shift
Start from an external drive	Command-Option-Shift-Delete
Eject a stuck CD or DVD	Hold down mouse button
Reset Parameter RAM	Command-Option-P-R

Screen-Capture Shortcuts

To do this action	Use this shortcut
Take a picture of the whole screen	Command-Shift-3
Take a picture of part of the screen	Command-Shift-4 and drag to select the area you want in the image
Take a picture of a window, the menu bar, or the Dock or other area	Command-Shift-4-spacebar; move the camera icon over the area you want to select and then click

Troubleshooting Shortcuts

To do this action	Use this shortcut
Stop a process	Command-period (.)
Force an application to quit	Command-Option-Esc
Force the computer to restart	Command-Control-Eject button

B

Resources

Like some things in life—having kids, for example, or rooting for the Red Sox—owning a Mac makes you part of a tight-knit community you barely knew existed before.

Mac users are a welcoming bunch, full of useful advice they gladly share. And here are some of the places Mac users go for information about their favorite computer.

News and Troubleshooting

MacCentral

http://maccentral.macworld.com

Look here for no-nonsense, timely Apple-industry news.

MacFixIt

www.macfixit.com

If your Mac is acting funny, check here. If someone else is having the same problem, chances are you can learn about it—and learn how to fix it—at MacFixIt.

MacInTouch

www.macintouch.com

A great site for Mac news, information, and analysis. At times, MacInTouch is almost an advocacy group for Mac users.

MacSlash

www.macslash.com

Similar to Slashdot, the popular programmers' discussion site, this Macintosh news and discussion forum is updated daily. It's good for finding out what loyal Mac users *really* think.

MacNN

www.macnn.com

Good, prompt news coverage with analysis.

MacWindows

www.macwindows.com

Focuses on making Macs and Windows machines work together.

Tidbits

www.tidbits.com

A wonderful online publication full of useful news and insights.

eWEEK.com

www.eweek.com

Not a Mac site, so listed last. This is the site I write my columns for, and we do a pretty good job of covering major Apple news without over-doing it. After all, we have lots of things to write about besides Apple. Most of my editors are not-so-secret Macheads.

Magazines

The Mac magazines can tend toward boosterism and at times seem to review some pretty useless products to fill pages.

MacAddict

www.macaddict.com

News, reviews, and how-tos with attitude.

MacDesign Magazine

www.macdesignonline.com

Useful ideas and tutorials for the hobbyist graphic designer as well as the more advanced designer.

MacDirectory

www.macdirectory.com

A directory of Mac software, along with news and reviews. Very stylish.

MacHome

www.machome.com

Magazine written for the personal—as opposed to professional—user.

MacTech

www.mactech.com

For users who want to and like to dig beyond the user level.

Macworld

www.macworld.com

The first Mac magazine and still the best.

Peachpit Press Books

Peachpit Press publishes a number of excellent books about the Macintosh and Mac applications. Here's a partial list:

Getting Started with Your Mac and Mac OS X Tiger: Peachpit Learning Series

Mac OS X 10.4 Tiger: Peachpit Learning Series

Mac OS X 10.4 Tiger: Visual QuickStart Guide

Mac OS X Help Line, Tiger Edition

Mac OS X Server 10.4 Tiger: Visual QuickPro Guide

Mac OS X Tiger Killer Tips

Take Control of Tiger

The Little Mac Book, Tiger Edition

The Robin Williams Mac OS X Book, Tiger Edition

Upgrading to Mac OS X 10.4 Tiger: Visual QuickProject Guide

Apple Sites

Apple Service & Support

www.apple.com/support

First stop for Apple's news, discussion groups, and software downloads.

Mac OS X

www.apple.com/macosx

Apple's home base for Mac OS X.

.Mac

www.mac.com

If you have a .Mac account, here's where you can get the latest software, participate in discussion groups, get support, access your Web mail, and more.

Switching

www.apple.com/switch

Apple helps you make the switch here—plus you get lots of testimonials.

Third-Party Software and Other Sites

dealmac

www.dealmac.com

Provides useful information on buying Apple and third-party products.

The Mac Orchard

www.macorchard.com

Clearinghouse for Internet-related applications for the Mac.

MacUpdate

www.macupdate.com

A comprehensive site for software updates.

Making the Macintosh

library.stanford.edu/mac

A tremendous online resource that documents the history of the Macintosh.

Mactopia

www.mactopia.com

News, updates, and support for Microsoft's Mac applications from Microsoft's Mac software division.

Small Dog Electronics

www.smalldog.com

The online Apple Store is a fine place to buy Mac products, but many swear by this site, too.

VersionTracker

www.versiontracker.com

Look here for an exhaustive list of Mac OS X software updates. Sometimes you can get a free membership as part of a .Mac membership. I use this site to keep my software up to date as well as to find new applications I might be interested in.

Index